Propel US Academy Guide to TOEFL
Step Ahead for TOEFL

OrangeBooks Publication

1st Floor, Rajhans Arcade, Mall Road, Kohka, Bhilai, Chhattisgarh 490020

Website:**www.orangebooks.in**

© Copyright, 2024, Author

All rights reserved. No part of this book may be reproduced, stored in a retrieval system, or transmitted, in any form by any means, electronic, mechanical, magnetic, optical, chemical, manual, photocopying, recording or otherwise, without the prior written consent of its writer.

First Edition, 2024

PROPEL US ACADEMY GUIDE TO
TOEFL

STEP AHEAD FOR TOEFL

SHUBHRA CHANPURIYA

OrangeBooks Publication
www.orangebooks.in

Content

What is the TOEFL? 1

Reading Section 3

Types Of Questions In The Reading Section 5

Practice Reading - 1 12
Title: Impact of Climate Change on Wildlife Populations

Practice Reading - 2 17
Title: The Benefits of Physical Exercise for Mental Health

Practice Reading - 3 21
Title: Renewable Sustainable Solution for the Future

Practice Reading - 4 26
Title: The Impact of Artificial Intelligence on the Job Market

Practice Reading - 5 31
Title: The Impact of Social Media on Society

Practice Reading - 6 36
Title: The Importance of Emotional Intelligence in the Workplace

Practice Reading - 7 41
Title: The Effects of Climate Change on Global Biodiversity

Practice Reading - 8 46
Title: The Benefits and Challenges of Remote Work

Practice Reading - 9 51
Title: The Impact of Social Media on Mental Health

Practice Reading - 10 56
Title: The Cultural Significance of Traditional Festivals

Listening Section 61

Practice Listening - 1 64
Title: The Pros and Cons of Technology in Education Transcript

Practice Listening - 2 67
Title: The Impact of Climate Change on Global Health Transcript

Practice Listening - 3 70
Title: The Impact of Artificial Intelligence on the Future Job Market Transcript

Practice Listening - 4 73
Title: The Impact of Social Media on Youth Mental Health Transcript

Practice Listening - 5 76
Title: The Advantages and Disadvantages of Online Learning Transcript

Practice Listening - 6 79
Title: The Impact of Deforestation on Climate Change Transcript

Practice Listening - 7 82
Title: The Importance of Renewable Energy Transcript

Practice Listening - 8 85
Title: The Benefits of Cultural Diversity Transcript

Practice Listening - 9 88
Title: The Importance of Early Childhood Education Transcript

Practice Listening - 10 91
Title: The Impact of Climate Change on Global Agriculture Transcript

Speaking Section 94

Speaking Task 1 Example - Opinion 96

Speaking Task 2 Example - Conversation 98

Speaking Task 3 Example - Academic Lecture 102

Sample Speaking Question - 1 106

Sample Speaking Question - 2 108

Sample Speaking Question - 3 110

Sample Speaking Question - 4 113

Sample Speaking Question - 5 115

Sample Speaking Question - 6 117

Sample Speaking Question - 7 119

Sample Speaking Question - 8 121

Sample Speaking Question - 9 123

Sample Speaking Question - 10 125

Writing Section 127

Sample Writing Question - 1 130

Sample Writing Question - 2 132

Sample Writing Question - 3 134

Sample Writing Question - 4 136

Sample Writing Question - 5 138

Sample Integrated Writing Task - 1 140

Sample Integrated Writing Task - 2 144

Sample Integrated Writing Task - 3 147

Sample Integrated Writing Task - 4 150

Sample Integrated Writing Task - 5 153

Grammar for the TOEFL 157

Vocabulary for the TOEFL 160

What is the TOEFL?

The TOEFL (Test of English as a Foreign Language) examination is an internationally recognized test used to measure non-native English speakers' proficiency in the English language. It assesses their ability to understand and use English in an academic setting such as English-speaking colleges. The TOEFL can be taken either as a computer-based or written test, with the computer-based format being more common.

The test consists of four sections: reading, listening, speaking, and writing in English. The reading section evaluates a test taker's ability to understand and analyze academic texts, while the listening section assesses their comprehension skills through audio recordings of academic lectures and conversations. The speaking section measures a test taker's ability to express their ideas verbally, while the writing section evaluates their ability to write coherent and well- structured essays. Each section is scored on a scale of 0 to 30 with a total of 0 to 120 for the entire exam.

To register for the TOEFL, test takers can visit the official TOEFL website www.ets.org/toefl or contact their local testing centers. The registration process typically involves providing personal information, selecting a test date and location, and paying the registration fee. It is recommended to register well in advance, as test dates can fill up quickly.

Testing areas for the TOEFL examination are available worldwide at authorized testing centers. These centers can be found in most major cities and are equipped with the necessary technology to administer the computer-based test. Test takers should ensure they bring valid identification documents on the test day, such as a passport or national ID.

The TOEFL examination holds relevance in various academic environments. It is commonly required for admission to English-speaking universities, especially for courses taught in English. Many government agencies and businesses also recognize the TOEFL as a reliable measure of English language proficiency.

This comprehensive study guide offers practice tests, sample questions, and detailed explanations of exam topics. It is advisable to allocate enough time for self-study and practice, focusing on all four sections of the exam. Familiarizing oneself with the test format, developing effective strategies, and building vocabulary and grammar skills are key elements for success in the TOEFL.

The Reading section consists of 3-4 passages with 10 questions each, lasting about 60-80 minutes. The Listening section comprises 4-6 lectures or conversations with 6 questions each and spans 60-90 minutes. The Speaking section includes 4 tasks, involving expressing opinions and summarizing information, and takes around 17 minutes. Lastly, the Writing section requires test-takers to complete 2 tasks, comprising writing an essay and summarizing information, within 50 minutes. There is a 10-minute break after the Reading and Listening sections. In total, the exam typically lasts about 3 hours and 10 minutes, excluding the break time.

Section	Question	Time
Reading	3-4 passages, 10-min each	60-80 min
Break		10 min
Listening	4-6 lectures, 6 questions each	60-90 min
Speaking	4 tasks	17 min
Writing	2 tasks	50 min
Total		**3 hr 10 min**

Scoring for the TOEFL exam ranges from 0 to 120, with each section worth a maximum of 30 points. The overall score is a combination of the individual section scores. Test-takers receive their scores approximately 10 days after completing the exam.

The pricing for the TOEFL exam varies depending on the country, but it generally ranges from $160 to $250. Additional fees may apply for services such as rescheduling or sending scores to multiple institutions.

Reading Section

How to master the reading section?

The Reading section of the TOEFL exam can be challenging for many test-takers, requiring a deep understanding of English reading comprehension skills. However, with effective strategies and diligent practice, individuals can enhance their performance and achieve success. This essay explores key tactics such as efficient note-taking, time management, recognizing the author's tone, understanding different types of questions, and other crucial reading comprehension strategies that can lead to improved scores in the TOEFL reading section.

Efficient Note-Taking

One essential strategy for excelling in the TOEFL reading section is efficient note-taking. While reading the passage, it is crucial to highlight or underline key information, such as main ideas, supporting details, and any important keywords. These notes can be invaluable when answering questions as they allow for quick reference and help maintain focus throughout the section.

Time Management

Time management is crucial in the TOEFL reading section, as test-takers often face tight time constraints. To optimize performance, it is essential to practice reading efficiently and quickly, without sacrificing comprehension. Skim through the passage first to get a general understanding before diving into the details. Allocate an appropriate amount of time to each question, ensuring that enough time is left for more challenging or time-consuming questions.

Recognizing the Author's Tone

Understanding the author's tone is vital for comprehending the nuances in a passage. By analyzing the author's attitude towards the subject, test-takers can better interpret the information and answer related questions accurately. Pay attention to the choice of words, the portrayal of characters or events, and any expressive language used by the author to determine their tone.

Comprehending Various Types of Questions

To excel in the TOEFL reading section, it is crucial to familiarize oneself with different types of questions that may be encountered. These include vocabulary questions, inference questions, main idea questions, supporting detail questions, and logical structure questions. Understanding the specific requirements of each question type and practicing them extensively will enhance the ability to identify the correct answers efficiently.

Active Reading Strategies

Implementing active reading strategies can significantly improve comprehension and performance in the reading section. Techniques such as predicting the passage's content based on the title or headings, summarizing paragraphs in one's own words, and making connections between ideas within the passage can help extract important information effectively. Active reading also involves engaging with the passage emotionally, intellectually, and critically, which aids in better understanding and retention of the content.

Utilizing Context Clues and Prior Knowledge

Effective use of context clues and prior knowledge can be immensely beneficial when encountering unfamiliar vocabulary or complex ideas. Context clues are clues provided within the passage that can help determine the meaning of unknown words or phrases. Additionally, drawing upon one's prior knowledge and personal experiences can aid in understanding the context better and provide useful insights when answering questions.

Success in the TOEFL reading section requires a combination of effective strategies and dedicated practice. Adopting tactics such as efficient note-taking, managing time effectively, recognizing the author's tone, comprehending various question types, engaging in active reading, and utilizing context clues and prior knowledge can significantly improve performance in this section. Consistent practice and exposure to a variety of reading materials will further enhance reading comprehension skills, leading to improved scores and overall success in the TOEFL examination.

Types Of Questions In The Reading Section

Inference

The Inference question type in the TOEFL Reading section tests a test-taker's ability to draw conclusions or make educated guesses based on information presented in the passage. These questions require critical thinking skills and the ability to go beyond the surface meaning of the text.

Inference questions often ask test-takers to make logical deductions, identify implicit information, or determine the author's intentions. They require a deep understanding of the passage and the ability to connect different parts of the text to arrive at a meaningful inference.

Sample Passage:

Excerpt from a TOEFL-style passage:

"In the late 19th century, the Industrial Revolution brought about significant changes to society. Factories sprang up, transforming the way goods were manufactured and distributed. As a result, urbanization increased as people flocked to cities in search of employment opportunities. However, these rapid changes also led to social upheaval and economic disparities."

Inference Question:

Based on the information provided in the passage, which of the following statements is most likely to be true?

    A. Urbanization decreased during the late 19th century.

    B. The Industrial Revolution had a minimal impact on society.

    C. Employment opportunities in rural areas were plentiful.

    D. Social upheaval and economic disparities were consequences of the rapid changes.

Correct Answer: D) Social upheaval and economic disparities were consequences of the rapid changes.

Explanation: This answer is correct because it directly reflects the information presented in the passage. The passage mentions that the Industrial Revolution led to social upheaval and economic disparities, making it the most likely true statement among the choices provided.

Vocabulary

The Vocabulary question type in the TOEFL Reading section assesses a test-taker's ability to understand and correctly interpret the meaning of specific words or phrases within the context of a passage. These questions require knowledge of a wide range of English vocabulary and the ability to understand how specific words are used in different contexts.

Vocabulary questions may ask test-takers to identify the meaning of a word based on its context, choose a synonym or antonym for a given word, or select the most appropriate word to replace a word or phrase in a sentence.

Sample Passage:

Excerpt from a TOEFL-style passage:

"The artist's work was characterized by its innovative use of color and form. His paintings were a juxtaposition of bold hues and subtle shades, creating a dynamic interplay of light and shadow."

Vocabulary Question:

In the passage, the word 'juxtaposition' most likely means:

    A. Similarity

    B. Division

    C. Comparison

    D. Placement

Correct Answer: C) Comparison

Explanation: In this context, 'juxtaposition' refers to the act of placing two things side by side in order to highlight their differences or similarities. Therefore, the correct answer is C) Comparison.

Main Idea

The Main Idea question type in the TOEFL Reading section evaluates a test-taker's ability to identify and comprehend the central theme or primary focus of a passage. These questions require the test-taker to have a clear understanding of the main point or purpose of the passage as a whole.

Main Idea questions typically ask test-takers to determine the overarching message or primary argument presented in the passage. They require the ability to discern the key points and themes while disregarding less important details.

Sample Passage:

Excerpt from a TOEFL-style passage:

"Climate change poses a significant threat to the planet, with rising temperatures leading to more frequent and severe natural disasters. Human activities, such as burning fossil fuels and deforestation, are major contributors to this environmental crisis. Urgent action is required to mitigate the impact of climate change and preserve the planet for future generations."

Main Idea Question:

What is the main idea of the passage?

    A. The effects of climate change on natural disasters

    B. Human activities causing climate change

    C. Urgent action needed to address climate change

    D. The importance of preserving the planet for future generations

Correct Answer: C) Urgent action needed to address climate change

Explanation: The main idea of the passage is that urgent action is required to address the impact of climate change. While the other options are mentioned in the passage, the central theme revolves around the need for immediate measures to mitigate the effects of climate change.

Supporting Detail

The Supporting Detail question type in the TOEFL Reading section tests a test-taker's ability to identify specific information that provides evidence or supports the main idea of a passage.

These questions require a close reading of the text to locate and understand the details that substantiate the central argument or theme.

Supporting Detail questions may ask test-takers to identify specific facts, examples, definitions, or descriptions that are directly related to the main idea or purpose of the passage. They require the ability to recognize how certain details contribute to the overall meaning of the text.

Sample Passage:

Excerpt from a TOEFL-style passage:

"The Industrial Revolution had a profound impact on society, ushering in an era of rapid technological advancements and urbanization. Factories replaced traditional modes of production, leading to increased efficiency and output. However, this period also saw the rise of social inequalities and labor exploitation as workers toiled in dangerous and unsanitary conditions."

Supporting Detail Question: According to the passage, what was a consequence of the Industrial Revolution?

    A. Increased efficiency and output

    B. Labor exploitation and social inequalities

    C. The rise of traditional modes of production

    D. Workers enjoying safe and sanitary conditions

Correct Answer: B) Labor exploitation and social inequalities

Explanation: The passage explicitly states that as a consequence of the Industrial Revolution, there was a rise in social inequalities and labor exploitation as workers endured dangerous and unsanitary conditions in the newly established factories. This detail directly supports the main idea of the passage.

Logical Structure

The Logical Structure question type in the TOEFL Reading section evaluates a test-taker's ability to understand the organization and flow of information within a passage. These questions assess the test-taker's comprehension of how ideas are connected, structured, and presented in the text.

Logical Structure questions may ask test-takers to identify the sequence of events, the relationship between different ideas or arguments, or the overall organization of the passage. They require the test-taker to recognize the logical progression of information and how each part contributes to the text as a whole.

Sample Passage:

Excerpt from a TOEFL-style passage:

"Overfishing has led to a decline in marine biodiversity and the depletion of fish stocks in oceans around the world. This environmental issue has far- reaching consequences not only for marine ecosystems but also for human populations that rely on fish as a source of food and livelihood. Sustainable fishing practices are essential to ensure the long-term health of marine ecosystems and the sustainability of fish populations."

Logical Structure Question: What is the relationship between overfishing and its consequences according to the passage?

    A. Overfishing has positive effects on marine biodiversity.

    B. Overfishing leads to a depletion of fish stocks and impacts human populations.

    C. Sustainable fishing practices are not necessary to address overfishing.

    D. Marine ecosystems are unaffected by overfishing.

Correct Answer: B) Overfishing leads to a depletion of fish stocks and impacts human populations.

Explanation: The passage establishes a clear cause and effect relationship between overfishing and its consequences, stating that overfishing leads to a decline in marine biodiversity, depletion of fish stocks, and impacts on human populations. This logical structure question requires understanding the sequence of events and the relationship between overfishing and its outcomes.

Function

The Function question type in the TOEFL Reading section assesses a test-taker's ability to understand the purpose or role of a specific sentence, paragraph, or passage within the context of the entire text. These questions require the test-taker to analyze how each part of the passage contributes to the overall meaning or structure.

Function questions may ask test-takers to determine the author's main intention, identify the argumentative strategy used, or understand the role of a particular piece of information in the passage. They require the ability to recognize the function and significance of various elements in the text.

Sample Passage:

Excerpt from a TOEFL-style passage:

"In the 21st century, technology has revolutionized the way people communicate and interact with one another. Social media platforms enable individuals to connect across borders and share information instantly. However, concerns about privacy and data security have emerged as technology companies collect and analyze user data for targeted advertising and other purposes."

Function Question: What is the function of the second paragraph in the passage?

    A. To explain the benefits of technology in communication

    B. To discuss the challenges of using social media platforms

    C. To highlight the ways technology has improved global connections

D. To introduce concerns related to privacy and data security

Correct Answer: D) To introduce concerns related to privacy and data security

Explanation: The function of the second paragraph is to introduce the concerns about privacy and data security that have emerged as a result of advancements in technology. This paragraph sets the stage for discussing potential drawbacks and implications of technological progress, highlighting the importance of considering these issues in the broader context of communication technologies.

Opinion

The Opinion question type in the TOEFL Reading section evaluates a test-taker's ability to recognize and interpret the author's subjective viewpoint or perspective on a particular issue or topic. These questions require the test-taker to differentiate between facts and opinions expressed in the passage.

Opinion questions may ask test-takers to identify the author's viewpoint, attitude, or stance on a given subject. They require the ability to discern subjective statements, evaluations, or judgments made by the author within the text.

Sample Passage:

Excerpt from a TOEFL-style passage:

"The government's decision to increase taxes on luxury goods has sparked a debate among economists and policymakers. Proponents argue that such measures are necessary to address income inequality and generate revenue for public services. Opponents, however, believe that higher taxes will discourage consumer spending and hinder economic growth."

Opinion Question: Based on the passage, what is the author's opinion on the government's decision to increase taxes on luxury goods?

    A. The author supports the decision as a means to address income inequality.

    B. The author opposes the decision, viewing it as detrimental to economic growth.

    C. The author is neutral and presents both sides of the argument equally.

    D. The author does not express a clear opinion on the issue.

Correct Answer: A) The author supports the decision as a means to address income inequality.

Explanation: The passage presents an argument in favor of increasing taxes on luxury goods to address income inequality and generate revenue. The author's opinion can be inferred from the viewpoint expressed by the proponents of the tax increase, indicating support for the decision as a means to achieve specific economic and social goals.

Purpose

The Purpose question type in the TOEFL Reading section tests a test-taker's ability to understand why the author has included specific information or details in the passage. These questions require the test-taker to identify the underlying intention or objective behind the author's writing.

Purpose questions may ask test-takers to determine the author's reason for including certain examples, arguments, or details in the passage. They require the ability to recognize the author's intended message, argumentative strategy, or communicative goal.

Sample Passage:

Excerpt from a TOEFL-style passage:

"The study of history provides valuable insights into the past and helps us understand the present and future. By examining historical events and their consequences, we can learn from past mistakes and successes, shaping our decisions and actions today. History serves as a mirror through which we can reflect on our society and ourselves."

Purpose Question: What is the main purpose of the passage?

    A. To demonstrate the importance of studying history

    B. To highlight the impact of historical events on society

    C. To explore the benefits of learning from past mistakes

    D. To explain how history shapes our decisions and actions

Correct Answer: A) To demonstrate the importance of studying history

Explanation: The main purpose of the passage is to underscore the significance of studying history as a means of gaining insights into the past, understanding the present, and shaping our future decisions and actions. The author's intention is to emphasize the value and relevance of historical knowledge in guiding our understanding of society and ourselves.

Practice Reading - 1

Title: Impact of Climate Change on Wildlife Populations

Passage:

Climate change has emerged as a significant global concern, affecting various aspects of our environment. Wildlife populations are particularly vulnerable to the rapid changes occurring in their habitats. Rising temperatures, altered precipitation patterns, and shifting ecosystems all contribute to the challenges faced by these species. The consequences of climate change on wildlife populations can be far-reaching, from shifts in migration patterns to changes in reproductive cycles and food availability. Thus, understanding the impact of climate change on wildlife is crucial for implementing effective conservation strategies.

Question 1:

What is the main topic of this passage?

    A. The impact of climate change on wildlife populations.

    B. The importance of conservation efforts.

    C. Climate change and its global effects.

    D. The challenges faced by wildlife in shifting ecosystems.

Correct answer: A) The impact of climate change on wildlife populations.

Explanation: The main topic of the passage is the impact of climate change specifically on wildlife populations. While it mentions conservation efforts and the global effects of climate change, these are discussed in relation to their impact on wildlife populations.

Question 2:

What does "vulnerable" mean in the context of the passage?

    A. Strong and resilient.

    B. Exposed to danger or harm.

    C. Adapted to changing conditions.

    D. Resistant to environmental changes.

Correct answer: B) Exposed to danger or harm.

Explanation: In the context of the passage, the word "vulnerable" refers to the idea that wildlife populations are at risk or easily harmed due to the rapid changes caused by climate change.

Question 3:

How are wildlife populations affected by climate change?

    A. Migration patterns remain unaffected.

    B. Reproductive cycles become more predictable.

    C. Food availability remains constant.

    D. Habitats and ecosystems undergo changes.

Correct answer: D) Habitats and ecosystems undergo changes.

Explanation: The passage states that wildlife populations are affected by climate change through changes in their habitats and ecosystems. Migration patterns, reproductive cycles, and food availability are also mentioned as specific consequences of these changes.

Question 4:

What is the purpose of understanding the impact of climate change on wildlife?

    A. To explore the relationship between climate change and migration patterns.

    B. To highlight the importance of global conservation efforts.

    C. To develop effective strategies for wildlife conservation.

    D. To identify the consequences of shifting ecosystems.

Correct answer: C) To develop effective strategies for wildlife conservation.

Explanation: The passage suggests that understanding the impact of climate change on wildlife is crucial in order to implement effective strategies for conservation. While the other options are mentioned in the passage, the main purpose mentioned is developing strategies for conservation.

Question 5:

Which term refers to a change in the timing of animal migrations?

    A. Altered precipitation patterns.

    B. Shifting ecosystems.

    C. Rising temperatures.

    D. Migration patterns.

Correct answer: D) Migration patterns.

Explanation: Migration patterns are specifically mentioned in the passage as being affected by climate change, indicating a change in timing.

Question 6:

What is the relationship between altered precipitation patterns and wildlife populations?

    A. Altered precipitation patterns do not impact wildlife populations.

    B. Altered precipitation patterns cause increased food availability.

    C. Altered precipitation patterns contribute to shifts in ecosystems.

    D. Altered precipitation patterns result in stable habitats.

Correct answer: C) Altered precipitation patterns contribute to shifts in ecosystems.

Explanation: The passage states that altered precipitation patterns, along with rising temperatures and shifting ecosystems, contribute to the challenges faced by wildlife populations. This suggests that altered precipitation patterns have a relationship with shifts in ecosystems.

Question 7:

Which phrase can be used to replace "far-reaching" without changing the meaning?

    A. Extensive

    B. Limited

    C. Superficial

    D. Insignificant

Correct answer: A) Extensive

Explanation: "Far-reaching" means having widespread impact or influence, and "extensive" carries a similar meaning, making it the appropriate choice.

Question 8:

According to the passage, what is crucial for implementing effective conservation strategies?

    A. Understanding the global effects of climate change.

    B. Recognizing the challenges faced by wildlife.

    C. Identifying reproductive cycles of endangered species.

    D. Understanding the impact of climate change on wildlife.

Correct answer: D) Understanding the impact of climate change on wildlife.

Explanation: The passage emphasizes the importance of understanding the impact of climate change on wildlife as crucial for implementing effective conservation strategies.

Question 9:

What is the author's primary objective in writing this passage?

    A. To raise awareness about the consequences of climate change.

    B. To analyze the factors contributing to wildlife population decline.

    C. To discuss specific conservation strategies for wildlife populations.

    D. To inform readers about the impact of climate change on ecosystems.

Correct answer: A) To raise awareness about the consequences of climate change.

Explanation: The passage aims to raise awareness about the impact of climate change on wildlife populations, emphasizing the need for understanding and implementing effective conservation strategies.

Question 10:

What phrase best represents the relationship between rising temperatures and the challenges faced by wildlife populations?

    A. Result in

    B. Lead to

    C. Exclude

    D. Prevent

Correct answer: B) Lead to

Explanation: The passage states that rising temperatures, along with other factors, contribute to the challenges faced by wildlife populations. The phrase "lead to" accurately represents this cause-and-effect relationship.

Practice Reading - 2

Title: The Benefits of Physical Exercise for Mental Health

Regular physical exercise is known to have numerous benefits for both physical and mental well-being. Engaging in physical activities such as jogging, swimming, or cycling not only improves cardiovascular health but also positively impacts mental health. Exercise stimulates the release of endorphins, which are natural mood-enhancing chemicals in the brain. Additionally, physical exercise reduces stress and promotes relaxation by lowering cortisol levels, the hormone associated with stress. The benefits of exercise on mental health are further underscored by its positive effects on sleep quality and overall brain function.

In terms of word meanings, one widely used term associated with exercise is "endorphins." What do endorphins refer to in the context of the passage?

    A. Mood-enhancing chemicals in the brain.

    B. Stress hormones released during exercise.

    C. Physical activities that improve cardiovascular health.

    D. Hormones associated with brain function.

Correct answer: A) Mood-enhancing chemicals in the brain.

Explanation: Endorphins are mentioned in the passage as natural mood-enhancing chemicals in the brain, highlighting their positive impact on mental well-being.

Which of the following is NOT a benefit of physical exercise on mental health, as discussed in the passage?

    A. Improved sleep quality.

    B. Reduced stress levels.

    C. Enhanced brain function.

    D. Increased cortisol production.

Correct answer: D) Increased cortisol production.

Explanation: The passage states that physical exercise reduces cortisol levels, which suggests that it does not lead to increased cortisol production. The other options are listed as benefits of exercise on mental health.

Based on the passage, why does physical exercise positively impact mental health?

    A. It promotes relaxation and releases mood-enhancing chemicals in the brain.

    B. It stimulates cortisol production and improves cardiovascular health.

    C. It heightens brain function and reduces sleep quality.

    D. It enhances stress levels and lowers endorphin levels.

Correct answer: A) It promotes relaxation and releases mood-enhancing chemicals in the brain.

Explanation: The passage highlights that physical exercise reduces stress, promotes relaxation, and stimulates the release of endorphins, which positively impact mental health.

What is the main idea of the passage?

    A. Physical exercise is essential for improving sleep quality.

    B. Endorphins are hormones associated with cardiovascular health.

    C. Physical exercise contributes to both physical and mental well-being.

    D. Cortisol is the primary hormone responsible for mood enhancement.

Correct answer: C) Physical exercise contributes to both physical and mental well-being.

Explanation: The passage focuses on the benefits of physical exercise for both physical and mental well-being, making it the main idea of the passage.

How does physical exercise help reduce stress levels?

    A. By stimulating cortisol production in the brain.

    B. By enhancing sleep quality and brain function.

    C. By promoting relaxation and lowering cortisol levels.

    D. By releasing mood-enhancing chemicals in the body.

Correct answer: C) By promoting relaxation and lowering cortisol levels.

Explanation: The passage states that physical exercise reduces stress and promotes relaxation by lowering cortisol levels, making option C the correct choice.

Which of the following statements is supported by the passage?

    A. Physical exercise only benefits cardiovascular health.

    B. Exercise has no impact on brain function.

    C. Mental health is unrelated to physical well-being.

    D. Exercise positively affects sleep quality.

Correct answer: D) Exercise positively affects sleep quality.

Explanation: The passage mentions that exercise not only improves cardiovascular health but also positively impacts mental health, including sleep quality.

What is the effect of exercise on overall brain function?

    A. It stimulates cortisol production, improving cognitive abilities.

    B. It has no impact on brain function.

    C. It enhances brain function.

    D. It reduces the production of endorphins.

Correct answer: C) It enhances brain function.

Explanation: The passage suggests that exercise positively affects overall brain function, so option C is the correct choice.

Based on the passage, what is the relationship between physical exercise and sleep quality?

    A. Exercise decreases sleep quality.

    B. Exercise has no impact on sleep quality.

    C. Exercise increases sleep quality.

    D. Exercise affects only cardiovascular health.

Correct answer: C) Exercise increases sleep quality.

Explanation: The passage states that physical exercise has positive effects on sleep quality, indicating a relationship between exercise and improved sleep.

Which of the following best represents the argument-evidence relationship in this passage?

    A. The benefits of exercise on mental health are widely recognized.

    B. Physical activities have positive impacts on physical and mental well-being.

    C. Exercise stimulates the release of endorphins, which improve mood.

D. Physical exercise reduces cortisol levels, a hormone associated with stress.

Correct answer: D) Physical exercise reduces cortisol levels, a hormone associated with stress.

Explanation: Option D presents the evidence (physical exercise reduces cortisol levels) that supports the argument presented in the passage (exercise has positive impacts on mental health).

Practice Reading - 3

Title: Renewable Sustainable Solution for the Future

In recent years, the use of renewable energy sources has gained significant attention as societies worldwide strive to combat climate change and reduce their dependence on fossil fuels.

Renewable energy refers to energy derived from sources that are naturally replenished, such as sunlight, wind, water, and geothermal heat. Unlike non-renewable energy sources like coal, oil, and gas, renewable energy offers numerous benefits and has the potential to revolutionize the way we generate and consume power.

One of the advantages of renewable energy is its contribution to reducing greenhouse gas emissions. Traditional forms of energy generation, such as burning fossil fuels, release massive amounts of carbon dioxide and other greenhouse gases, contributing to global warming and climate change. Renewable energy sources, on the other hand, produce little to no greenhouse gas emissions during operation. By transitioning to renewable energy, societies can significantly decrease their carbon footprint and mitigate the adverse effects of climate change.

Another crucial benefit of renewable energy is its potential for energy independence. Most countries heavily rely on imported fossil fuels for their energy needs, which can have economic and geopolitical implications. By diversifying their energy mix and promoting the use of renewable sources, countries can become less dependent on foreign fossil fuels. This not only provides energy security but also stimulates local economies by creating jobs in the renewable energy sector.

Additionally, renewable energy promotes sustainable development and environmental stewardship. Unlike fossil fuel extraction, which often disrupts ecosystems and causes environmental damage, renewable energy projects can be designed to minimize habitat destruction and preserve biodiversity. Moreover, renewable energy sources are virtually inexhaustible, ensuring a long-term and sustainable energy supply for future generations.

Renewable energy technologies have seen remarkable advancements in recent years. Solar power, for instance, has become more efficient and affordable, with solar panels now being widely utilized in residential, commercial, and industrial settings. Wind turbines have also become more efficient, tapping into strong winds to generate large amounts of electricity. Furthermore, innovative developments in tidal and wave power, as well as geothermal systems, are showing promise in harnessing the Earth's natural resources for sustainable energy generation.

While the benefits of renewable energy are evident, challenges remain in widespread adoption. The initial cost of renewable energy systems and infrastructure can be prohibitive, requiring significant investments. However, as technology advances and economies of scale are achieved, the cost of renewable energy is projected to continue decreasing. Additionally, the intermittent nature of some renewable energy sources, such as wind and solar, poses challenges for grid stability and energy storage. However, advancements in energy storage technologies, such as batteries, are addressing these issues and ensuring a more reliable and balanced energy supply.

In conclusion, renewable energy offers a sustainable and cleaner alternative to traditional energy sources. The advantages of reducing greenhouse gas emissions, promoting energy independence, fostering sustainable development, and advancing technological innovations make renewable energy essential for a greener future. With continued advancements and investments, renewable energy has the potential to reshape the global energy landscape, paving the way for a more sustainable and resilient world.

Multiple Choice Questions:

What is the main focus of this passage?

    A. The environmental impact of renewable energy sources.

    B. The economic implications of renewable energy adoption.

    C. The challenges facing renewable energy implementation.

    D. The benefits of renewable energy for sustainable development.

Correct answer: D) The benefits of renewable energy for sustainable development.

Explanation: The passage primarily discusses the advantages and benefits of renewable energy sources and their role in sustainable development.

According to the passage, what distinguishes renewable energy sources from non-renewable energy sources?

    A. The availability of subsidies for renewable energy.

    B. The level of greenhouse gas emissions released during operation.

C. The geographical location where the energy sources are found.

D. The average cost per unit of energy produced.

Correct answer: B) The level of greenhouse gas emissions released during operation.

Explanation: The passage mentions that renewable energy sources produce little to no greenhouse gas emissions during operation, distinguishing them from non-renewable energy sources.

What is the primary advantage of transitioning to renewable energy sources?

A. Mitigating the adverse effects of climate change.

B. Diversifying the energy mix of a country.

C. Ensuring energy security through domestic production.

D. Creating job opportunities in the energy sector.

Correct answer: A) Mitigating the adverse effects of climate change.

Explanation: The passage states that the primary advantage of transitioning to renewable energy is their contribution to reducing greenhouse gas emissions, thus mitigating the adverse effects of climate change.

Based on the passage, why is energy independence important?

A. To ensure a steady supply of fossil fuels.

B. To create jobs in the renewable energy sector.

C. To minimize the reliance on foreign energy sources.

D. To decrease the cost of energy production.

Correct answer: C) To minimize the reliance on foreign energy sources.

Explanation: The passage mentions that energy independence can be achieved by promoting renewable energy sources, reducing the dependence on foreign fossil fuels.

Which statement best reflects the passage's viewpoint on renewable energy technologies?

A. They have reached their peak and are unlikely to improve further.

B. They require large-scale changes in infrastructure and technology.

C. They have seen significant advancements in recent years.

D. They are limited to solar and wind energy sources.

Correct answer: C) They have seen significant advancements in recent years.

Explanation: The passage mentions that renewable energy technologies have witnessed remarkable advancements, providing examples like solar power, wind turbines, tidal and wave power, and geothermal systems.

What is identified as a challenge to the widespread adoption of renewable energy?

   A. The limited availability of subsidies for renewable energy projects.

   B. The high cost of renewable energy systems and infrastructure.

   C. The intermittent nature of renewable energy sources.

   D. The lack of technological advancements in energy storage.

Correct answer: B) The high cost of renewable energy systems and infrastructure.

Explanation: The passage highlights the initial cost of renewable energy systems and infrastructure as a challenge to their widespread adoption.

Which statement BEST reflects the passage's view on the future of renewable energy?

   A. Renewable energy will replace all traditional energy sources in the near future.

   B. The intermittent nature of renewable energy sources cannot be overcome.

   C. Continued advancements will make renewable energy more affordable and reliable.

   D. The reliance on foreign fossil fuels will persist due to economic constraints.

Correct answer: C) Continued advancements will make renewable energy more affordable and reliable.

Explanation: The passage suggests that as technology advances and economies of scale are achieved, the cost of renewable energy is expected to decrease, making it more affordable and reliable in the future.

Based on the passage, what is one possible solution to address the intermittent nature of renewable energy sources?

   A. Increasing subsidies for renewable energy projects.

   B. Relying on non-renewable energy sources for grid stability.

   C. Advancements in energy storage technologies, such as batteries.

   D. Limiting the use of renewable energy to residential areas.

Correct answer: C) Advancements in energy storage technologies, such as batteries.

Explanation: The passage mentions that advancements in energy storage technologies, like batteries, are addressing the issues related to the intermittent nature of renewable energy sources.

Overall, the passage suggests that renewable energy is:

    A. Cost-prohibitive and inefficient compared to fossil fuels.

    B. Limited in its environmental benefits.

    C. Essential for a greener and more sustainable future.

    D. Insufficient to meet the world's growing energy needs.

Correct answer: C) Essential for a greener and more sustainable future.

Explanation: The passage emphasizes the advantages and potential of renewable energy in creating a greener and more sustainable future.

What is the main purpose of the passage?

    A. To discuss the challenges facing renewable energy implementation.

    B. To advocate for the adoption of renewable energy sources.

    C. To analyze the economic implications of renewable energy.

    D. To explore the advancements of renewable energy technologies.

Correct answer: B) To advocate for the adoption of renewable energy sources.

Explanation: The passage aims to highlight the benefits and advantages of renewable energy sources, advocating for their adoption and emphasizing their importance for a sustainable future.

Practice Reading - 4

Title: The Impact of Artificial Intelligence on the Job Market

In recent years, artificial intelligence (AI) has emerged as a transformative technology that is reshaping various sectors of the global economy. While AI presents numerous opportunities for innovation and efficiency, its widespread adoption has also raised concerns about its impact on the job market. As AI capabilities continue to advance, there is a growing fear that automation will lead to significant job displacement.

AI has already begun to automate routine and repetitive tasks across industries, resulting in increased productivity and cost savings for businesses. This trend is expected to continue, with AI systems becoming more sophisticated and capable of performing complex cognitive tasks. While automation may eliminate certain jobs, it also creates new opportunities for workers to take on more challenging and fulfilling roles.

One of the areas most affected by AI is the manufacturing sector, where robots and intelligent machines can perform tasks with exceptional precision and speed. This has led to the displacement of low-skilled workers who were previously responsible for routine assembly line tasks. However, it has also led to the emergence of new job roles such as robot programmers, technicians, and AI experts who are needed to develop, operate, and maintain these automated systems.

The impact of AI is not limited to the manufacturing sector. AI-powered software and algorithms have also made their way into fields like customer service, healthcare, finance, and transportation. Chatbots and virtual assistants are increasingly used to handle customer inquiries and provide assistance, reducing the need for human customer service representatives. In healthcare, AI algorithms are being utilized to diagnose diseases, analyze medical images, and provide personalized treatment plans. While these advancements streamline processes and improve accuracy, they may also reduce the demand for certain healthcare professionals.

It is important to note that while jobs may be displaced by automation, new job opportunities emerge as well. The development and implementation of AI systems require skilled professionals who understand the technology and can design, maintain, and improve AI algorithms. As AI becomes more prevalent, demand for these technical roles is expected to increase. Moreover, AI can enhance productivity and competitiveness, leading to the growth of existing industries and the emergence of new ones, creating a demand for a broad range of skills.

The impact of AI on the job market also depends on the ability of workers to adapt and acquire new skills. As automation becomes more commonplace, there is a growing need for workers to develop a combination of technical and soft skills that complement AI capabilities. Skills such as critical thinking, creativity, problem-solving, and emotional intelligence are increasingly valued and can enhance job prospects in an AI-driven economy.

Governments and educational institutions play a crucial role in preparing the workforce for the AI revolution. Investment in educational programs that equip individuals with AI-related skills and promote lifelong learning can help bridge the skills gap. Additionally, policies that promote job reskilling and upskilling, as well as social safety nets to support workers affected by automation, are necessary to ensure a smooth transition in the job market.

In conclusion, AI has the potential to greatly impact the job market by automating routine tasks and creating new opportunities. While certain jobs may be displaced, the emergence of new roles and the demand for AI-related skills present opportunities for workers to adapt and thrive.

Governments, businesses, and individuals must work together to harness the potential of AI while ensuring the workforce is prepared for the changing landscape of work.

Multiple Choice Questions:

What is the main focus of this passage?

    A. The advancements of artificial intelligence technology.

    B. Job displacement caused by artificial intelligence.

    C. The potential of artificial intelligence in various industries.

    D. The need for AI-related skills in the workforce.

Correct answer: B) Job displacement caused by artificial intelligence.

Explanation: The main focus of the passage is the impact of artificial intelligence on the job market, particularly the concern of job displacement due to automation.

How does automation impact the manufacturing sector?

    A. It leads to the displacement of low-skilled workers.

    B. It creates new job roles related to robotics and AI.

    C. It increases productivity and cost savings for businesses.

    D. All of the above.

Correct answer: D) All of the above.

Explanation: The passage states that automation in the manufacturing sector leads to the displacement of low-skilled workers, the creation of new job roles, and increased productivity and cost savings for businesses.

What role does AI play in customer service?

    A. AI reduces the need for human customer service representatives.

    B. AI enhances the accuracy of customer service interactions.

    C. AI improves customer satisfaction.

    D. All of the above.

Correct answer: D) All of the above.

Explanation: The passage mentions that AI-powered chatbots and virtual assistants are used to handle customer inquiries, reducing the need for human representatives and improving accuracy, leading to enhanced customer satisfaction.

According to the passage, what skills are increasingly valued in an AI-driven economy?

    A. Technical skills related to artificial intelligence.

    B. Soft skills such as critical thinking and problem-solving.

    C. Both technical and soft skills.

    D. Emotional intelligence.

Correct answer: C) Both technical and soft skills.

Explanation: The passage highlights that in an AI-driven economy, a combination of technical skills related to AI and soft skills such as critical thinking, creativity, problem-solving, and emotional intelligence are increasingly valued.

How does the impact of AI on the job market depend on workers?

    A. Workers need to adapt to acquiring new skills.

    B. Workers need to become experts in AI development.

C. Workers need to compete with AI systems.

D. Workers need to prioritize job security.

Correct answer: A) Workers need to adapt to acquiring new skills.

Explanation: The passage highlights the importance of workers adapting and acquiring new skills to complement AI capabilities in order to thrive in the changing job market.

What role do governments and educational institutions play in the AI revolution?

A. Developing AI systems to replace human workers.

B. Creating policies to limit the impact of AI on jobs.

C. Investing in educational programs to equip individuals with AI-related skills.

D. Providing financial support to businesses affected by automation.

Correct answer: C) Investing in educational programs to equip individuals with AI-related skills.

Explanation: The passage states that governments and educational institutions play a crucial role by investing in educational programs that equip individuals with AI-related skills and promoting lifelong learning.

What is the main purpose of the passage?

A. To explore the potential of artificial intelligence.

B. To advocate for the adoption of AI in various industries.

C. To discuss the challenges posed by artificial intelligence.

D. To analyze the impact of artificial intelligence on the job market.

Correct answer: D) To analyze the impact of artificial intelligence on the job market.

Explanation: The main purpose of the passage is to analyze and discuss the impact of artificial intelligence on the job market, including the concerns of job displacement and the need for new skills.

How can the growth of existing industries and the emergence of new ones be fueled by AI?

A. By replacing human workers with AI systems.

B. By eliminating the need for skilled professionals.

C. By enhancing productivity and competitiveness.

D. By stifling innovation and creativity.

Correct answer: C) By enhancing productivity and competitiveness.

Explanation:: The passage states that AI can enhance productivity and competitiveness, leading to the growth of existing industries and the emergence of new ones.

What does the passage suggest about the future job market?

    A. AI will completely replace human workers.

    B. The demand for AI-related skills will decrease.

    C. Workers need to develop a combination of technical and soft skills.

    D. There will be no job opportunities due to automation.

Correct answer: C) Workers need to develop a combination of technical and soft skills.

Explanation:: The passage suggests that in the future job market, workers need to develop a combination of technical and soft skills to complement AI capabilities.

What is the impact of AI on the job market according to the passage?

    A. It will lead to widespread unemployment.

    B. It will create new job opportunities.

    C. It will only affect low-skilled workers.

    D. It will primarily benefit large corporations.

Correct answer: B) It will create new job opportunities.

Explanation:: The passage mentions that while certain jobs may be displaced by AI, it also creates new opportunities for workers to take on more challenging roles.

Practice Reading - 5

Title: The Impact of Social Media on Society

Social media has revolutionized the way people communicate and interact with one another. Platforms such as Facebook, Instagram, Twitter, and Snapchat have become integral parts of daily life for billions of users worldwide. While social media offers numerous benefits, its impact on society is a subject of ongoing debate.

One of the significant impacts of social media is its ability to connect people from different corners of the globe. Through these platforms, individuals can easily communicate with friends, family, and even strangers, breaking down geographical barriers. This connectivity has resulted in the sharing of diverse perspectives and cultural exchange, fostering a sense of global community.

However, social media's impact extends beyond connectivity. Its influence on mental health has become a growing concern. Studies have shown a correlation between social media usage and negative psychological effects such as increased feelings of loneliness, anxiety, and depression. The constant exposure to carefully curated and idealized versions of others' lives can create unrealistic expectations and foster a sense of inadequacy in individuals.

Moreover, social media has influenced the way information is disseminated and consumed. The rise of "fake news" and misinformation has become a prevalent issue, fueled by the ability of information to spread rapidly. The ease of sharing content, often without proper fact-checking, has resulted in the dissemination of false information and the polarization of public opinion. This challenges the credibility of traditional news sources and raises questions about the role of social media platforms in facilitating a reliable information ecosystem.

Another area of concern is the impact of social media on privacy. The collection and use of personal data by social media companies raise questions about individual privacy rights. The monetization of user data and targeted advertising further blur the line between personal and corporate interests, leading to debates around issues of consent and data protection.

However, it is important to note that social media also plays a significant role in social activism and awareness. Movements such as #MeToo and #BlackLivesMatter gained traction and mobilized support through social media platforms. Social media has provided a platform for marginalized voices to be heard and has facilitated the spread of information and discussions on important social issues.

In conclusion, social media has both positive and negative impacts on society. It connects people across the globe, fosters a sense of community, and allows for the exchange of ideas. However, it also presents challenges such as negative effects on mental health, the spread of misinformation, and concerns surrounding privacy. To maximize the benefits of social media while minimizing its drawbacks, individuals and society as a whole must be mindful of its impact and engage in responsible and critical usage.

Multiple Choice Questions:

What is the main topic of this passage?

    A. The impact of social media on mental health.

    B. The benefits of social media.

    C. The negative effects of social media on society.

    D. The role of social media in social activism.

Correct answer: C) The negative effects of social media on society.

Explanation:: The main topic of the passage is the impact of social media on society, with a specific focus on the negative effects.

What is one positive impact of social media mentioned in the passage?

    A. Increased feelings of loneliness and depression.

    B. Polarization of public opinion.

    C. Promotion of cultural exchange.

    D. Challenges to privacy rights.

Correct answer: C) Promotion of cultural exchange.

Explanation:: The passage mentions that social media platforms have facilitated the sharing of diverse perspectives and cultural exchange, thus promoting understanding and a sense of global community.

What negative impact of social media is mentioned in the passage?

    A. Increased connectivity.

    B. Spread of misinformation.

    C. Mobilization of social activism.

    D. Facilitation of social interactions.

Correct answer: B) Spread of misinformation.

Explanation:: The passage mentions that social media has led to the rise of "fake news" and the dissemination of misinformation, which is a negative impact on society.

How does social media impact mental health, according to the passage?

    A. It promotes feelings of loneliness and inadequacy.

    B. It fosters a sense of global community.

    C. It improves communication and connectivity.

    D. It enables social activism and awareness.

Correct answer: A) It promotes feelings of loneliness and inadequacy.

Explanation:: The passage states that social media usage has been correlated with negative psychological effects such as increased feelings of loneliness, anxiety, and depression.

What is one concern related to the impact of social media on privacy?

    A. The ease of sharing content.

    B. The role of social media platforms in facilitating information dissemination.

    C. The collection and use of personal data by social media companies.

    D. The monetization of user data.

Correct answer: C) The collection and use of personal data by social media companies.

Explanation:: The passage mentions that the collection and use of personal data by social media companies raise concerns about individual privacy rights.

What role does social media play in social activism, according to the passage?

    A. It fosters feelings of loneliness and inadequacy.

    B. It amplifies the spread of misinformation.

    C. It challenges privacy standards.

    D. It provides a platform for marginalized voices.

Correct answer: D) It provides a platform for marginalized voices.

Explanation:: The passage mentions that social media platforms have played a significant role in social activism by providing a platform for marginalized voices to be heard and facilitating discussions on important social issues.

What is the writer's overall view of social media?

    A. Social media has only negative impacts on society.

    B. The negative effects of social media outweigh the positive benefits.

    C. Social media has positive and negative impacts on society.

    D. The positive impacts of social media outweigh the negative effects.

Correct answer: C) Social media has positive and negative impacts on society.

Explanation: The writer acknowledges that social media has both positive and negative impacts on society, as mentioned throughout the passage.

What does the passage suggest about responsible social media usage?

    A. Individuals should avoid using social media entirely.

    B. Social media platforms should take responsibility for misinformation.

    C. Society needs to be mindful of the impact of social media and use it critically.

    D. Users should prioritize privacy protection over connectivity.

Correct answer: C) Society needs to be mindful of the impact of social media and use it critically.

Explanation:: The passage suggests that individuals and society as a whole should be aware of the impact of social media and engage in responsible and critical usage.

How does social media connect people, according to the passage?

    A. By fostering a sense of global community.

    B. By enabling the spread of misinformation.

    C. By promoting cultural exchange.

    D. By negatively impacting mental health.

Correct answer: A) By fostering a sense of global community.

Explanation: The passage mentions that social media platforms facilitate connectivity by allowing individuals to communicate and interact across geographical barriers, fostering a sense of global community.

What is the main purpose of this passage?

    A. To analyze the positive impact of social media on society.

    B. To advocate for the responsible use of social media.

    C. To promote the use of social media for social activism.

    D. To explore the influence of social media on mental health.

Correct answer: B) To advocate for the responsible use of social media.

Explanation: The passage aims to discuss the impact of social media on society, addressing both the positive and negative effects, and ultimately advocates for responsible usage.

Practice Reading - 6

Title: The Importance of Emotional Intelligence in the Workplace

In today's professional environment, technical skills and qualifications are no longer the sole determinants of success. Employers recognize the significance of emotional intelligence (EQ) in the workplace and value employees who possess this essential trait. Emotional intelligence refers to a person's ability to perceive, understand, and manage their own emotions and the emotions of others.

One of the fundamental aspects of emotional intelligence is self-awareness. Individuals with high EQ possess the ability to recognize and understand their own emotions, strengths, weaknesses, and limitations. This self-awareness allows them to effectively manage their behavior, response to stress, and interpersonal relationships.

Additionally, emotional intelligence plays a crucial role in interpersonal relationships and communication. Employees with high EQ are skillful in recognizing and understanding the emotions of others, leading to effective communication and fostering positive working relationships. They can navigate conflicts and difficult conversations with empathy, actively listen to others, and adapt their communication style to suit different situations and personalities.

Moreover, emotional intelligence is strongly linked to leadership abilities. Leaders with high EQ are perceived as more approachable, empathetic, and effective in managing teams. They can inspire and motivate their team members, resolve conflicts, and create a positive work environment. The ability to understand and meet the emotional needs of employees is critical in building trust and loyalty within the team.

Research has shown that higher levels of emotional intelligence contribute to numerous positive outcomes in the workplace. Employees with high EQ tend to experience lower levels of stress, better job satisfaction, and higher levels of overall well-being. They are also more resilient in the face of challenges and setbacks, able to adapt to change, and display better decision-making skills.

The importance of emotional intelligence is particularly evident in customer service roles. Employees who possess high EQ can effectively manage difficult customers, defuse conflicts, and provide exceptional customer experiences. They can empathize with customers' needs and concerns, leading to superior customer satisfaction and loyalty.

However, it is essential to note that emotional intelligence can be developed and strengthened over time. It is not solely an innate trait but can be cultivated through practice and self-reflection. Employers can play a vital role in promoting emotional intelligence within the workplace by providing training and fostering a supportive and inclusive culture that encourages open communication and empathy.

In conclusion, emotional intelligence is a critical factor in achieving success in the workplace. It contributes to effective communication, interpersonal relationships, leadership abilities, and overall well-being. Employers recognize the value of emotional intelligence and seek employees who possess not only technical skills but also the ability to understand and manage their own emotions and the emotions of others. By cultivating emotional intelligence, individuals can enhance their professional growth, contribute to a positive work environment, and thrive in their careers.

Multiple Choice Questions:

What is the main focus of this passage?

    A. The benefits of technical skills in the workplace.

    B. The link between emotional intelligence and job satisfaction.

    C. The importance of empathy in customer service roles.

    D. The significance of emotional intelligence in the workplace.

Correct answer: D) The significance of emotional intelligence in the workplace.

Explanation: The main focus of the passage is the importance of emotional intelligence in the workplace and its impact on various aspects of professional success.

What does emotional intelligence refer to?

    A. Technical skills and qualifications.

    B. The ability to perceive and understand one's own emotions.

    C. The ability to navigate conflicts and difficult conversations.

    D. The ability to inspire and motivate team members.

Correct answer: B) The ability to perceive and understand one's own emotions.

Explanation: The passage defines emotional intelligence as a person's ability to perceive, understand, and manage their own emotions and the emotions of others.

Which aspect of emotional intelligence is essential in managing interpersonal relationships?

    A. Self-management.

    B. Self-awareness.

    C. Empathy.

    D. Effective communication.

Correct answer: C) Empathy.

Explanation: The passage mentions that emotional intelligence plays a crucial role in effective interpersonal relationships, with individuals who possess high EQ being skillful in recognizing and understanding the emotions of others.

What is the connection between emotional intelligence and leadership abilities?

    A. Emotional intelligence is irrelevant to leadership.

    B. Leaders with high EQ are perceived as more approachable and effective.

    C. Leaders are resolute and unemotional.

    D. Emotional intelligence leads to better decision-making skills only.

Correct answer: B) Leaders with high EQ are perceived as more approachable and effective.

Explanation: The passage states that leaders with high emotional intelligence are perceived as more approachable, empathetic, and effective in managing teams, emphasizing the connection between emotional intelligence and leadership abilities.

According to the passage, which positive outcomes are associated with higher levels of emotional intelligence?

    A. Increased levels of stress and dissatisfaction.

    B. Improved decision-making skills and adaptability.

    C. Decreased overall well-being and job satisfaction.

    D. Higher levels of job satisfaction and overall well-being.

Correct answer: D) Higher levels of job satisfaction and overall well-being.

Explanation: The passage mentions that employees with high emotional intelligence tend to experience lower levels of stress, better job satisfaction, and higher levels of overall well-being.

How can emotional intelligence benefit customer service roles?

    A. It enables employees to handle difficult customers effectively.

    B. It eliminates the need for customer service representatives.

    C. It prevents conflicts and promotes a positive work environment.

    D. It improves decision-making skills.

Correct answer: A) It enables employees to handle difficult customers effectively.

Explanation: The passage states that employees with high emotional intelligence can effectively manage difficult customers, defuse conflicts, and provide exceptional customer experiences.

What is an important consideration regarding emotional intelligence mentioned in the passage?

    A. Emotional intelligence is solely an innate trait.

    B. Emotional intelligence cannot be developed or strengthened.

    C. Emotional intelligence can be learned and cultivated over time.

    D. Emotional intelligence is limited to specific professional roles.

Correct answer: C) Emotional intelligence can be learned and cultivated over time.

Explanation: The passage highlights that emotional intelligence is not solely an innate trait but can be developed and strengthened through practice and self-reflection.

How can employers promote emotional intelligence in the workplace?

    A. By disregarding the importance of emotional intelligence.

    B. By providing technical skills training exclusively.

    C. By promoting a supportive and inclusive culture.

    D. By reducing the emphasis on effective communication.

Correct answer: C) By promoting a supportive and inclusive culture.

Explanation: The passage mentions that employers can promote emotional intelligence within the workplace by fostering a supportive and inclusive culture that encourages open communication and empathy.

What is the writer's overall view of emotional intelligence?

    A. Emotional intelligence is unnecessary in the workplace.

    B. The benefits of emotional intelligence outweigh its drawbacks.

    C. Emotional intelligence is an innate trait and cannot be learned.

    D. Soft skills are more valuable than emotional intelligence.

Correct answer: B) The benefits of emotional intelligence outweigh its drawbacks.

Explanation: The writer acknowledges and emphasizes the benefits and significance of emotional intelligence in the workplace, suggesting that the benefits outweigh any potential drawbacks.

What is the main purpose of this passage?

    A. To analyze the impact of emotional intelligence on workplace productivity.

    B. To explore the relevance of technical skills in the workplace.

    C. To discuss the challenges associated with emotional intelligence in leadership.

    D. To highlight the importance of emotional intelligence in professional success.

Correct answer: D) To highlight the importance of emotional intelligence in professional success.

Explanation: The passage aims to highlight and emphasize the importance of emotional intelligence in professional success, particularly its impact on various aspects of the workplace.

Practice Reading - 7

Title: The Effects of Climate Change on Global Biodiversity

Climate change represents one of the most severe threats to global biodiversity. Rising temperatures, changing precipitation patterns, and increased frequency of extreme weather events are altering ecosystems and causing significant disruptions to wildlife populations. As these changes continue, it becomes increasingly crucial to understand the effects of climate change on biodiversity and implement effective conservation strategies.

One of the primary impacts of climate change on biodiversity is habitat loss and fragmentation. Many species are adapted to specific climatic conditions and rely on stable habitats to survive and reproduce. However, as temperatures shift and ecosystems change, habitats become unsuitable for some species, forcing them to shift their geographic ranges or face extinction. This loss of suitable habitat can result in biodiversity decline and disrupt ecosystem functioning.

In addition to habitat loss, climate change also affects species interactions and ecological relationships. Synchronized timing between species, such as flowering plants and their pollinators or predator-prey interactions, can be disrupted due to shifts in seasonal patterns. This misalignment can have cascading effects on entire ecosystems. For instance, if the timing of flowering plants and their pollinators is no longer synchronized, it can impact the reproductive success of both plant and pollinator species and potentially disrupt the entire food web.

Climate change also poses challenges to species that are highly specialized or limited in their habitat and resource requirements. These species are often less adaptable to rapid environmental changes and may face difficulties in finding suitable habitats or food sources. Climate change can increase competition among species as they seek limited resources, leading to increased vulnerability for some populations.

Furthermore, climate change exacerbates other existing threats to biodiversity, such as habitat degradation, pollution, and invasive species. Rising temperatures can favor the spread and proliferation of invasive species, which can outcompete native species for resources and disrupt ecological balance. Additionally, as climate change amplifies water scarcity and alters water availability, freshwater ecosystems and their dependent species face significant challenges.

Mitigating the impacts of climate change on biodiversity requires a multifaceted approach that encompasses conservation efforts, sustainable land and water management practices, and international collaboration. Conservation strategies should focus on protecting existing habitats, restoring degraded ecosystems, and creating wildlife corridors that facilitate the movement of species. It is also crucial to enhance the resilience of ecosystems and promote the conservation of species that are highly vulnerable to climate change.

Public awareness and education about climate change and its impact on biodiversity are essential for fostering a sense of responsibility and inspiring actions for change. Governments, businesses, and individuals play a critical role in reducing greenhouse gas emissions, transitioning to renewable energy sources, and adopting sustainable practices that minimize the ecological footprint.

In conclusion, climate change poses significant threats to global biodiversity, including habitat loss, disruptions to species interactions, and increased vulnerability for specialized species.

These impacts have cascading effects on ecosystems and ecosystem services. By implementing conservation strategies, raising awareness, and adopting sustainable practices, we can mitigate the impacts of climate change on biodiversity and work towards a more sustainable future.

Multiple Choice Questions:

What is the main focus of this passage?

    A. The impact of climate change on wildlife populations.

    B. The importance of biodiversity for ecosystem functioning.

    C. The challenges of habitat loss and fragmentation.

    D. The role of international collaboration in conservation.

Correct answer: A) The impact of climate change on wildlife populations.

Explanation: The main focus of the passage is the impact of climate change on global biodiversity, with a specific emphasis on wildlife populations.

What is one primary effect of climate change on biodiversity mentioned in the passage?

    A. Decreased competition among species.

B. Increased resilience of ecosystems.

C. Disruptions in species interactions and ecological relationships.

D. Reduced habitat degradation and pollution.

Correct answer: C) Disruptions in species interactions and ecological relationships.

Explanation: The passage mentions that climate change can disrupt the synchronized timing between species and ecological relationships, leading to cascading effects on ecosystems.

How does climate change exacerbate other threats to biodiversity?

A. By decreasing competition among species.

B. By accelerating the spread of invasive species.

C. By reducing the vulnerability of specialized species.

D. By promoting sustainable land and water management practices.

Correct answer: B) By accelerating the spread of invasive species.

Explanation: The passage mentions that rising temperatures can favor the spread of invasive species, which can outcompete native species, leading to disruptions in ecosystems.

According to the passage, what can be the impact of misaligned timing between flowering plants and pollinators?

A. Increased reproductive success for both plant and pollinator species.

B. Disruption of the entire food web.

C. Enhanced adaptation to climate change.

D. Decreased significance of specialized species.

Correct answer: B) Disruption of the entire food web.

Explanation: The passage states that misaligned timing between flowering plants and their pollinators can impact the reproductive success of both species and potentially disrupt the entire food web.

How does climate change affect species that are highly specialized or limited in their habitat requirements?

A. Climate change favors the adaptation of these species.

B. These species face increased competition for limited resources.

C. Climate change increases the range of habitat for these species.

    D. These species become more adaptable to rapid environmental changes.

Correct answer: B) These species face increased competition for limited resources.

Explanation: The passage mentions that climate change can increase competition among species, particularly for limited resources, resulting in increased vulnerability for specialized species.

What is one recommended approach for mitigating the impacts of climate change on biodiversity?

    A. Protecting existing habitats and creating wildlife corridors.

    B. Increasing the vulnerability of specialized species.

    C. Reducing public awareness of climate change and its impact.

    D. minimizing the importance of renewable energy sources.

Correct answer: A) Protecting existing habitats and creating wildlife corridors.

Explanation: The passage suggests that protecting existing habitats, restoring degraded ecosystems, and creating wildlife corridors are recommended approaches for mitigating the impacts of climate change on biodiversity.

What is the writer's overall view of climate change's impact on biodiversity?

    A. Climate change has little to no impact on global biodiversity.

    B. The challenges of climate change can be easily overcome.

    C. Climate change poses significant threats to global biodiversity.

    D. Climate change primarily benefits specialized species.

Correct answer: C) Climate change poses significant threats to global biodiversity.

Explanation: The writer's overall view, as presented in the passage, is that climate change represents one of the most severe threats to global biodiversity.

Which action is NOT mentioned as a way to mitigate the impacts of climate change on biodiversity?

    A. Adopting sustainable practices to minimize the ecological footprint.

    B. Enhancing the resilience of ecosystems.

    C. Conserving species that are highly vulnerable to climate change.

    D. Ignoring public awareness and education about climate change.

Correct answer: D) Ignoring public awareness and education about climate change.

Explanation: The passage mentions that public awareness and education about climate change and its impact on biodiversity are essential for fostering a sense of responsibility and inspiring action for change.

What parallel is drawn between emotional intelligence and climate change?

    A. Emotional intelligence can contribute to global warming.

    B. Emotional intelligence is irrelevant to the workforce.

    C. Climate change is as important as emotional intelligence.

    D. The impact of climate change is as severe as emotional intelligence.

Correct answer: C) Climate change is as important as emotional intelligence.

Explanation: There is no parallel drawn between emotional intelligence and climate change in the passage. This statement is not supported.

What is the main purpose of this passage?

    A. To explore the challenges of climate change.

    B. To advocate for international collaboration in conservation efforts.

    C. To discuss the importance of biodiversity for global ecosystems.

    D. To analyze the effects of climate change on global biodiversity.

Correct answer: D) To analyze the effects of climate change on global biodiversity.

Explanation: The main purpose of the passage is to analyze and discuss the effects of climate change on global biodiversity, including the challenges and necessary conservation strategies.

Practice Reading - 8

Title: The Benefits and Challenges of Remote Work

Remote work, also known as telecommuting or working from home, has gained significant popularity in recent years. Enabled by advances in technology, remote work offers numerous benefits for both employees and employers. However, it also presents unique challenges that need to be addressed for remote work to be sustainable and effective.

One of the primary benefits of remote work is increased flexibility. Employees have the freedom to work from any location, allowing for a better work-life balance. This flexibility can lead to higher job satisfaction, reduced commute times, and increased productivity. Additionally, remote work can attract and retain top talent, as it offers the opportunity for individuals to work for companies regardless of geographical location.

Another advantage of remote work is cost savings. Both employees and employers can save on commuting costs, office space expenses, and other associated overheads. Remote work can also contribute to a reduced carbon footprint, as it eliminates the need for daily commuting, resulting in environmental benefits.

Furthermore, remote work can enhance diversity and inclusivity in the workplace. By eliminating geographical barriers, companies can tap into a global talent pool, promoting diversity and inclusion. Remote work can also foster a more inclusive work environment by accommodating individuals with disabilities or caregiving responsibilities who may face challenges in traditional office settings.

However, remote work also comes with challenges that need to be addressed. One such challenge is the potential for decreased work-life boundaries. Working from home can blur the line between work and personal life, leading to longer working hours and difficulty in disconnecting. It is essential for individuals to establish clear boundaries and develop healthy work habits to maintain a healthy work-life balance.

Another challenge is the potential for decreased social interaction and collaboration. Remote work may lead to feelings of isolation, as employees miss out on the social interactions and informal connections that occur in a physical office setting. Remote workers may also face communication challenges, as they rely heavily on digital communication platforms. Companies need to prioritize fostering a sense of community and connection among remote workers through virtual team-building activities and regular check-ins.

Additionally, remote work can also require a higher degree of self-motivation and discipline. Working from home requires individuals to manage their time effectively, prioritize tasks, and stay focused amidst potential distractions in the home environment. Self-motivation and strong time management skills are critical for maintaining productivity and meeting deadlines.

Cybersecurity is another area of concern in remote work. With employees accessing company networks and sensitive information from their personal devices and home networks, the risk of data breaches and cyber-attacks increases. It is essential for companies to establish robust cybersecurity protocols and provide training to remote workers to ensure data security.

Despite the challenges, remote work is expected to continue growing in popularity. To make remote work sustainable and effective, companies need to invest in the necessary technological infrastructure, provide support for remote employees, and establish clear policies and guidelines.

Furthermore, remote work should be viewed as a flexible option rather than a one-size-fits-all solution, as some roles and industries may require physical presence or face-to-face interaction.

In conclusion, remote work offers numerous benefits such as increased flexibility, cost savings, and enhanced diversity and inclusivity. However, it comes with unique challenges that need to be addressed, including work-life boundaries, social interaction, self-motivation, and cybersecurity concerns. By understanding and proactively addressing these challenges, companies can capitalize on the benefits of remote work and create a productive and fulfilling remote work environment.

Multiple Choice Questions:

What is the main focus of this passage?

    A. The benefits of working from home.

    B. The challenges of remote work.

    C. The flexibility of remote work.

    D. The growth of remote work during recent years.

Correct answer: B) The challenges of remote work.

Explanation: The main focus of the passage is the challenges associated with remote work, although it also discusses the benefits.

What is one primary benefit of remote work mentioned in the passage?

    A. Improved work-life balance.

    B. Increased commuting times.

    C. Limited job satisfaction.

    D. Enhanced in-person collaboration.

Correct answer: A) Improved work-life balance.

Explanation: The passage mentions that remote work offers increased flexibility, which leads to a better work-life balance for employees.

How does remote work contribute to cost savings?

    A. It reduces employee productivity.

    B. It eliminates the need for office space.

    C. It requires additional commuting expenses.

    D. It increases overhead expenses for employers.

Correct answer: B) It eliminates the need for office space.

Explanation: The passage states that both employees and employers can save on office space expenses, among other associated overheads, through remote work.

What challenge is associated with remote work according to the passage?

    A. Increased in-person collaboration.

    B. Decreased social interaction and collaboration.

    C. Limited access to a global talent pool.

    D. Lower job satisfaction.

Correct answer: B) Decreased social interaction and collaboration.

Explanation: The passage mentions that remote work may lead to feelings of isolation and decreased social interaction, as employees miss out on the social interactions and informal connections that occur in a physical office setting.

What challenge does remote work pose to work-life balance?

    A. Increased work productivity.

    B. Difficulty in disconnecting from work.

C. Reduced commuting times.

D. Limited cost savings.

Correct answer: B) Difficulty in disconnecting from work.

Explanation: The passage states that remote work can blur the line between work and personal life, leading to longer working hours and difficulty in disconnecting, potentially affecting work- life balance.

What is one challenge related to cybersecurity mentioned in the passage?

A. Decreased productivity in remote work.

B. Increased carbon footprint due to remote work.

C. Potential data breaches and cyberattacks in remote work.

D. Reduced motivation in remote work.

Correct answer: C) Potential data breaches and cyberattacks in remote work.

Explanation: The passage mentions that with employees accessing company networks and sensitive information from their personal devices and home networks, the risk of data breaches and cyber-attacks increases.

What is one recommendation mentioned in the passage for making remote work effective?

A. Providing training to remote workers for data security.

B. Reducing flexibility in remote work options.

C. Investing in office space for remote employees.

D. Eliminating the need for digital communication platforms.

Correct answer: A) Providing training to remote workers for data security.

Explanation: The passage mentions that it is essential for companies to establish robust cybersecurity protocols and provide training to remote workers to ensure data security.

How does the passage suggest making remote work sustainable and effective?

A. By eliminating remote work options.

B. By prioritizing in-person collaboration.

C. By establishing clear policies and guidelines.

D. By reducing work flexibility.

Correct answer: C) By establishing clear policies and guidelines.

Explanation: The passage suggests that companies can make remote work sustainable and effective by establishing clear policies and guidelines, among other necessary measures.

What is one recommendation mentioned in the passage for companies to foster social interaction among remote workers?

    A. Limiting virtual team-building activities.

    B. Decreasing communication platforms for remote workers.

    C. Establishing a supportive and inclusive culture.

    D. Reducing check-ins with remote workers.

Correct answer: C) Establishing a supportive and inclusive culture.

Explanation: The passage suggests that companies need to prioritize fostering a sense of community and connection among remote workers through virtual team-building activities and regular check-ins.

What is the main purpose of this passage?

    A. To discuss the challenges of working from home.

    B. To advocate for in-person collaboration in the workplace.

    C. To analyze the benefits of remote work.

    D. To explore the benefits and challenges of remote work.

Correct answer: D) To explore the benefits and challenges of remote work.

Explanation: The main purpose of the passage is to explore and discuss the benefits and challenges associated with remote work.

Practice Reading - 9

Title: The Impact of Social Media on Mental Health.

The rise of social media has transformed the way people connect and communicate, offering numerous benefits such as extended social networks and increased access to information. However, there is growing concern about the impact of social media on mental health, particularly among young people. Research suggests that prolonged and excessive use of social media can contribute to negative psychological effects and exacerbate existing mental health issues.

One of the primary ways in which social media affects mental health is through the comparison of oneself to others. Social media platforms are often filled with carefully curated and idealized versions of people's lives, creating a distorted perception of reality. This constant exposure to highlight reels can lead to feelings of inadequacy, loneliness, and anxiety as individuals compare their lives to the seemingly perfect lives portrayed on social media.

Moreover, social media can contribute to increased levels of stress and anxiety. The constant pressure to curate a desirable online image, accumulate followers, and gain approval through likes and comments can create a sense of performance anxiety. The fear of missing out (FOMO) and the constant need to be connected can also lead to heightened stress levels and a sense of social exclusion.

Furthermore, the addictive nature of social media can have detrimental effects on mental health. Studies have related excessive social media use to symptoms of addiction, such as withdrawal, anxiety, and difficulty focusing. The constant need for validation and the instant gratification provided by social media platforms can lead to addictive behaviors and a decreased ability to regulate one's emotions.

Social media can also contribute to cyberbullying and negative online experiences. The anonymity provided by social media platforms can embolden individuals to engage in harmful behaviors, resulting in online harassment, cyberbullying, and the spread of hate speech. These negative experiences can have profound effects on an individual's mental well-being, contributing to feelings of depression, anxiety, and low self-esteem.

However, it is essential to recognize that social media is not inherently negative for mental health. It can also serve as a powerful tool for support, validation, and community-building. Online support groups and mental health communities can provide a sense of belonging and understanding, offering valuable support to individuals experiencing mental health challenges. Social media can also raise awareness about mental health issues, promote acceptance, and facilitate open discussions.

To mitigate the negative impact of social media on mental health, it is crucial to establish healthy digital habits. Setting limits on social media use, engaging in offline activities, and cultivating meaningful relationships outside of social media are essential for maintaining a balanced and healthy lifestyle. Being mindful of one's emotions and mental well-being while using social media is also crucial, as it allows individuals to engage critically with the content they consume and recognize the potential impact on their mental health.

Additionally, social media platforms and users themselves can take steps to promote mental well-being. Implementing features that encourage positive interactions, provide mental health resources, and combat cyberbullying can create safer and more supportive online environments. Users can actively promote positivity, authenticity, and kindness in their online interactions, contributing to a healthier social media ecosystem.

In conclusion, while social media offers unparalleled connectivity and information sharing, its impact on mental health should not be overlooked. The comparison culture, stress, addiction, and negative online experiences associated with social media can have detrimental effects on mental well-being. However, with mindful use, healthy digital habits, and collective efforts to promote mental well-being online, social media can be harnessed as a tool for support, community- building, and raising awareness about mental health issues.

Multiple Choice Questions:

What is the main focus of this passage?

- A. The benefits of social media for mental health.
- B. The addictive nature of social media.
- C. The impact of social media on mental health.
- D. The importance of online support groups.

Correct answer: C) The impact of social media on mental health.

Explanation: The main focus of the passage is to discuss the impact of social media on mental health, including the negative effects and some potential positive aspects.

What is one way in which social media affects mental health, according to the passage?

    A. Increased levels of stress and anxiety.

    B. Decreased levels of loneliness and inadequacy.

    C. Enhanced self-esteem and self-worth.

    D. Reduced fear of missing out (FOMO).

Correct answer: A) Increased levels of stress and anxiety.

Explanation: The passage mentions that the constant pressure and need for validation on social media can create increased levels of stress and anxiety.

What can be an effect of excessive social media use?

    A. Increased mental well-being and emotional regulation.

    B. Decreased levels of addiction and withdrawal symptoms.

    C. Symptoms of addiction, such as withdrawal and anxiety.

    D. Improved ability to regulate one's emotions.

Correct answer: C) Symptoms of addiction, such as withdrawal and anxiety.

Explanation: The passage mentions that excessive social media use has been related to symptoms of addiction, including withdrawal, anxiety, and difficulty focusing.

What is one negative effect of social media mentioned in the passage?

    A. Increased levels of social connectedness.

    B. Improved self-esteem and mental well-being.

    C. Cyberbullying and negative online experiences.

    D. Facilitation of open discussions on mental health.

Correct answer: C) Cyberbullying and negative online experiences.

Explanation: The passage mentions that social media can contribute to cyberbullying and negative online experiences, which can have profound effects on mental well-being.

According to the passage, how can social media be a positive tool for mental health?

    A. It can increase feelings of loneliness and inadequacy.

    B. It can contribute to high levels of stress and anxiety.

    C. It can provide support, validation, and community.

D. It can exacerbate symptoms of addiction.

Correct answer: C) It can provide support, validation, and community.

Explanation: The passage mentions that social media can serve as a powerful tool for support and community-building, providing valuable support to individuals experiencing mental health challenges.

What is one recommendation mentioned in the passage for mitigating the negative impact of social media on mental health?

- A. Engaging solely in online activities.
- B. Setting limits on social media use.
- C. Promoting comparison culture on social media.
- D. Decreasing offline activities.

Correct answer: B) Setting limits on social media use.

Explanation: The passage suggests setting limits on social media use as one way to mitigate the negative impact of social media on mental health.

What can social media platforms do to promote mental well-being online?

- A. Implementing features that encourage positive interactions and offer mental health resources.
- B. Encouraging increased screen time for users.
- C. Promoting cyberbullying and harassment.
- D. Reducing user engagement on their platforms.

Correct answer: A) Implementing features that encourage positive interactions and offer mental health resources.

Explanation: The passage mentions that social media platforms can implement features that encourage positive interactions, provide mental health resources, and combat cyberbullying, contributing to a healthier online environment.

What is the writer's overall view of social media's impact on mental health?

- A. Social media has no impact on mental well-being.
- B. The negative impacts of social media outweigh the potential benefits.
- C. Social media has primarily positive effects on mental health.
- D. The impact of social media on mental health varies depending on use.

Correct answer: D) The impact of social media on mental health varies depending on use.

Explanation: The writer's overall view, as presented in the passage, is that the impact of social media on mental health varies depending on individual use and the approaches taken by social media platforms and users themselves.

What is one possible action users can take to promote mental well-being on social media?

    A. Prioritizing comparison culture and seeking validation online.

    B. Engaging in performative behaviors for validation.

    C. Cultivating authenticity and kindness in online interactions.

    D. Decreasing their online presence on social media platforms.

Correct answer: C) Cultivating authenticity and kindness in online interactions.

Explanation: The passage suggests that users can actively promote positivity, authenticity, and kindness in their online interactions, contributing to a healthier social media ecosystem.

What is the main purpose of this passage?

    A. To analyze the impact of social media on mental health.

    B. To advocate for the elimination of social media platforms.

    C. To explore the limits of social media for mental health support.

    D. To discuss the benefits of social media for mental well-being.

Correct answer: A) To analyze the impact of social media on mental health.

Explanation: The main purpose of the passage is to analyze and discuss the impact of social media on mental health, including both the negative effects and potential positive aspects.

Practice Reading - 10

Title: The Cultural Significance of Traditional Festivals.

Traditional festivals play a vital role in preserving and celebrating cultural heritage across the globe. These festivals are deeply rooted in history, customs, and beliefs, and serve as important occasions for communities to come together, pass down traditions, and express their shared identity. They provide a unique insight into the diversity and richness of different cultures, fostering a sense of unity and pride among participants.

One of the primary purposes of traditional festivals is to commemorate significant historical events or religious occasions. These festivals often have deep historical significance, symbolizing important milestones or commemorating religious figures. Through rituals, processions, and artistic performances, communities honor and remember their past, reinforcing cultural identity and transmitting historical knowledge to future generations.

Traditional festivals also serve as opportunities for cultural exchange and dialogue. They attract visitors from different regions and even countries, providing a platform for intercultural interaction and understanding. Participants have the chance to learn about different customs, traditions, and ways of life, fostering mutual respect and appreciation for diverse cultures.

Moreover, traditional festivals showcase a wide array of artistic expressions, including music, dance, visual arts, and culinary traditions. These festivals serve as a stage for local artists and artisans to showcase their skills and creativity, preserving and promoting traditional art forms. From vibrant parades to intricate costumes and unique culinary delights, these festivals immerse participants in the cultural aesthetics and sensory experiences of a particular community.

Furthermore, traditional festivals strengthen social bonds and community cohesion. They bring people together in a shared space, encouraging social interactions and fostering a sense of belonging. Festivals often include activities that promote community participation, such as communal meals, traditional games, and collaborative performances. These shared experiences create lasting memories and strengthen the social fabric of a community.

However, despite their cultural significance, traditional festivals face several challenges in a rapidly changing world. Globalization, urbanization, and modernization have led to the erosion of traditional practices and the commercialization of some festivals. Pressure to attract tourists and generate revenue can sometimes result in the dilution or distortion of cultural traditions, undermining their authenticity and meaning.

Additionally, the fast-paced and demanding nature of modern life can make it difficult for individuals to fully engage in traditional festivals and pass down cultural practices to younger generations. Time constraints, changing lifestyles, and limited knowledge about cultural heritage can contribute to a decline in participation and understanding of traditional festivals.

To address these challenges and ensure the preservation of traditional festivals, efforts are being made at local, national, and international levels. Governments and cultural organizations are investing in the safeguarding and promotion of intangible cultural heritage, which includes traditional festivals. Inclusive policies and initiatives are being implemented to encourage community participation, knowledge transmission, and the revitalization of cultural traditions.

Education and awareness play a crucial role in the preservation and appreciation of traditional festivals. Schools and educational institutions can integrate cultural heritage into their curricula, allowing students to learn about and experience traditional festivals firsthand. Public awareness campaigns and cultural events can help raise appreciation and understanding among both locals and tourists.

In conclusion, traditional festivals hold immense cultural significance, serving as important occasions to celebrate, preserve, and pass down cultural heritage. They commemorate historical events, foster cultural exchange, showcase artistic expressions, and strengthen social cohesion. However, the preservation of these festivals faces challenges in a rapidly changing world. By investing in cultural preservation, promoting community participation, and raising awareness, societies can ensure that traditional festivals continue to thrive and contribute to the cultural richness of communities globally.

Multiple Choice Questions:

What is the main focus of this passage?

    A. The commercialization of traditional festivals.

    B. The historical significance of traditional festivals.

    C. The challenges faced by traditional festivals.

    D. The diversity of traditional festivals across different cultures.

Correct answer: C) The challenges faced by traditional festivals.

Explanation: The main focus of this passage is on the challenges faced by traditional festivals, although it also discusses their cultural significance.

What is one primary purpose of traditional festivals mentioned in the passage?

    A. To promote commercial interests.

    B. To foster community cohesion and social bonds.

    C. To attract tourists and generate revenue.

    D. To showcase international intercultural exchanges.

Correct answer: B) To foster community cohesion and social bonds.

Explanation: The passage mentions that traditional festivals bring people together, encouraging social interactions and fostering a sense of belonging, thus promoting community cohesion and social bonds.

What does the passage suggest about the role of traditional festivals in cultural preservation?

    A. Traditional festivals are no longer relevant in modern society.

    B. Traditional festivals have led to the erosion of cultural practices.

    C. Traditional festivals contribute to the preservation of cultural heritage.

    D. Cultural preservation is not a concern for traditional festivals.

Correct answer: C) Traditional festivals contribute to the preservation of cultural heritage.

Explanation: The passage suggests that traditional festivals play a vital role in preserving and passing down cultural heritage.

What can be viewed as a potential challenge to traditional festivals?

    A. The dilution or distortion of cultural traditions.

    B. The decline in participation due to lack of interest.

    C. The lack of collaboration and artistic expression.

    D. The focus on educational integration of traditional festivals.

Correct answer: A) The dilution or distortion of cultural traditions.

Explanation: The passage mentions that pressure to attract tourists and generate revenue can result in the dilution or distortion of cultural traditions.

What is one recommendation mentioned in the passage to address the challenges faced by traditional festivals?

   A. Increasing the commercialization of traditional festivals.

   B. Reducing community participation in traditional festivals.

   C. Investing in the safeguarding and promotion of cultural heritage.

   D. Decreasing awareness of the importance of cultural traditions.

Correct answer: C) Investing in the safeguarding and promotion of cultural heritage.

Explanation: The passage suggests that investing in the safeguarding and promotion of cultural heritage can address the challenges faced by traditional festivals.

What role can education play in the preservation of traditional festivals?

   A. Eliminating traditional festivals from school curricula.

   B. Raising awareness and appreciation for traditional festivals.

   C. Reducing community participation in traditional festivals.

   D. Limiting knowledge transmission about cultural heritage.

Correct answer: B) Raising awareness and appreciation for traditional festivals.

Explanation: The passage suggests that schools and educational institutions can integrate cultural heritage into their curricula, allowing students to learn about and experience traditional festivals firsthand, thus raising awareness and appreciation.

What is the writer's overall view of traditional festivals?

   A. Traditional festivals are inconsequential to cultural heritage preservation.

   B. The challenges faced by traditional festivals are insurmountable.

   C. Traditional festivals hold immense cultural significance.

   D. The commercialization of traditional festivals is necessary for their survival.

Correct answer: C) Traditional festivals hold immense cultural significance.

Explanation: The writer's overall view, as presented in the passage, is that traditional festivals hold immense cultural significance and play a vital role in preserving and passing down cultural heritage.

What is the primary purpose of this passage?

   A. To recommend the elimination of traditional festivals.

   B. To explore the artistic expressions showcased in traditional festivals.

C. To analyze the economic impact of traditional festivals.

D. To discuss the cultural significance of traditional festivals and the challenges they face.

Correct answer: D) To discuss the cultural significance of traditional festivals and the challenges they face.

Explanation: The primary purpose of this passage is to discuss the cultural significance of traditional festivals and the challenges they face, including potential solutions.

According to the passage, traditional festivals serve as a platform for what?

A. Cultural preservation and appreciation.

B. Interactions with tourists.

C. Economic growth for local communities.

D. The erosion of cultural practices.

Correct answer: A) Cultural preservation and appreciation.

Explanation: The passage mentions that traditional festivals are deeply rooted in history, customs, and beliefs, serving as important occasions for communities to come together, pass down traditions, and express their shared identity, thus preserving and appreciating cultural heritage.

What can be one potential negative consequence of the commercialization of traditional festivals?

A. Increased community participation.

B. The strengthening of traditional practices.

C. The dilution or distortion of cultural traditions.

D. A deeper sense of belonging and social cohesion.

Correct answer: C) The dilution or distortion of cultural traditions.

Explanation: The passage mentions that the pressure to attract tourists and generate revenue can result in the dilution or distortion of cultural traditions, undermining their authenticity and meaning.

Listening Section

How to master the listening section?

The Listening section of the TOEFL exam plays a crucial role in assessing an individual's ability to comprehend spoken English in an academic setting. Lasting between 60-90 minutes, this section consists of multiple recordings or lectures, and test-takers must answer a variety of question types, including main idea, detail, function, opinion, inference-based, and organization questions. To excel in this section, it is essential to employ effective strategies and be aware of common issues that may arise during the test. This essay outlines key details of the Listening section along with top strategies from reputable sources.The Listening section typically spans 60-90 minutes, during which test-takers navigate through several audio passages. The TOEFL Listening section generally includes four to six recordings or lectures. The section encompasses various question types, each assessing different listening skills: a. Main Idea Questions: These require identifying the central theme or main point of an audio passage. b.

Detail Questions: Test-takers must discern specific information mentioned in the audio. c. Function Questions: These assess the purpose or intention behind certain actions or statements in the audio. d. Opinion Questions: Test-takers are expected to identify the speaker's viewpoint or attitude on a particular topic. e. Inference-based Questions: These questions demand using reasoning and contextual clues to arrive at a conclusion. f. Organization Questions: Test-takers must understand the logical order of ideas or events presented in the audio.

Strategies for Excelling in the Listening Section

1. **Active Listening Techniques:**
   - Take notes while listening to aid comprehension and retain key information.
   - Focus on identifying keywords and phrases that convey pivotal information.
   - Pay attention to intonation, stress, and emphasis, as they often indicate important points.

2. Improve Vocabulary and Understanding:
- Enhance vocabulary by reading academic texts, listening to lectures, and engaging in English conversations.
- Familiarize yourself with common idiomatic expressions and phrasal verbs.
- Practice listening to different accents and speech rates to accustom yourself to diversity.

3. Utilize Available Time Optimally:
- Prior to listening to the recording/lecture, quickly skim through the related questions to have an idea of what to expect.
- Take advantage of the provided introductory information about the audio before it begins.

4. Monitor Time Management:
- Remain conscious of the time limit for each section, allocating sufficient time for answering questions.
- If a particular question seems difficult, it is advisable to move on and return to it later to avoid losing valuable time.

After the conversation and Common Issues:

1. What to Expect after the Conversation:
- Test-takers usually have 10-15 seconds to prepare and check their answers before moving on to the next question.
- It is essential to pace oneself, as the next audio passage starts automatically.

2. Common Issues to be Alert For:
- Multiple speakers: Be attentive to the roles and relationships between speakers.
- Negatives and conditional statements: Pay close attention to words that negate or conditionally modify statements.
- Transitions and signposting words: Understand how transition words and phrases link ideas or indicate changes in topic.

The Listening section of the TOEFL exam demands sharp listening skills and effective strategies. By employing active listening techniques, expanding vocabulary and comprehension abilities, managing time efficiently, and being alert to common challenges, test-takers can enhance their performance on this section. Regular practice, exposure to diverse accents, and familiarity with various question types are key to achieving success in the TOEFL Listening section.

Practice Listening - 1

Title: The Pros and Cons of Technology in Education
Transcript

Presenter: Good morning, everyone. Today, we will discuss the advantages and disadvantages of technology in education. Technology has become an integral part of our lives, transforming the way we learn, teach, and interact with information. In this lecture, we will explore both the benefits and drawbacks of incorporating technology in educational settings.

Let's dive into this important topic and examine the impact of technology in education.

Presenter: One of the major advantages of technology in education is its ability to enhance access to information. Through internet connectivity and digital resources, students and educators can access a vast amount of information from around the world. This access to information empowers learners to explore their interests, conduct research, and deepen their understanding of various subjects.

Presenter: Another benefit is the potential for interactive and engaging learning experiences. Technology provides tools such as multimedia presentations, simulations, and virtual reality that can make learning more interactive and immersive. This can foster student engagement and improve understanding and retention of complex concepts.

Presenter: However, technology in education also presents certain challenges. One notable drawback is the potential for technology to be a distraction. With access to devices like smartphones and tablets, students may be tempted to engage in non-educational activities during class, diverting their attention from the lesson at hand.

Presenter: Additionally, there is a concern about the potential for technology to widen the digital divide. In some areas or among certain population groups, access to technology and reliable internet connectivity may be limited or nonexistent. This can create inequalities in educational opportunities and hinder the learning experiences of those who do not have access to necessary technology resources.

Thank you for listening to today's lecture on the pros and cons of technology in education. We hope you gained valuable insights into the benefits and challenges associated with utilizing technology in educational settings.

Question 1:

What is the main topic of this lecture?

    A. The benefits of traditional teaching methods

    B. The challenges of integrating technology in education

    C. The impact of technology on student engagement

    D. The advantages and disadvantages of technology in education

Explanation: The correct answer is d) The advantages and disadvantages of technology in education. This question evaluates the test-taker's ability to comprehend and identify the main focus of the lecture. The presenter explicitly states that the lecture will explore both the benefits and drawbacks of incorporating technology in education.

Question 2:

What is one advantage of technology in education mentioned in the lecture?

    A. Limited access to information and resources

    B. Enhancement of student distractions

    C. Improved understanding and retention of complex concepts

    D. Widening of the digital divide

Explanation: The correct answer is c) Improved understanding and retention of complex concepts. This question measures the test-taker's comprehension skills. The presenter explains that technology can provide tools such as multimedia presentations and simulations to make learning more interactive and immersive, ultimately improving understanding and retention of complex concepts.

Question 3:

What is one concern mentioned regarding technology in education?

    A. Increased student engagement and focus

    B. Limited access to technology and internet connectivity

    C. Enhanced learning experiences from non-educational activities

    D. Elimination of traditional teaching methods

Explanation: The correct answer is b) Limited access to technology and internet connectivity. This question assesses the test-taker's comprehension skills. The presenter highlights that disparities in access to technology and reliable internet connectivity can create inequalities in educational opportunities.

Question 4:

What is one potential drawback mentioned in the lecture regarding technology in education?

    A. The potential for technology to enhance student distractions

    B. Increased opportunities for collaborative learning

    C. Improved access to digital resources and information

    D. Enhanced student engagement and motivation

Explanation: The correct answer is a) The potential for technology to enhance student distractions. This question evaluates the test-taker's comprehension skills. The presenter mentions that with access to devices like smartphones and tablets, students may be tempted to engage in non-educational activities during class, creating a potential distraction.

Question 5:

Based on the lecture, why is the digital divide a concern in relation to technology in education?

    A. It limits students from engaging in non-educational activities

    B. It promotes traditional teaching methods over technology use

    C. It hinders access to necessary technology resources and opportunities

    D. It eliminates distractions and increases student focus

Explanation: The correct answer is c) It hinders access to necessary technology resources and opportunities. This question assesses the test-taker's inference skills. Although not explicitly mentioned, the lecture emphasizes that the digital divide can create inequalities in educational opportunities due to limited or nonexistent access to technology and reliable internet connectivity.

Practice Listening - 2

Title: The Impact of Climate Change on Global Health Transcript

Presenter: Good morning, everyone. Today, we will discuss the impact of climate change on global health. Climate change, driven by human activities, has far-reaching consequences for the well-being of individuals and communities worldwide. In this lecture, we will explore the connection between climate change and various health challenges. Let's dive into this urgent topic and understand the implications of climate change on global health.

Presenter: One of the significant impacts of climate change on health is the increase in extreme weather events. Rising temperatures contribute to more frequent and severe heatwaves, which can result in heat-related illnesses and even death. Additionally, changes in precipitation patterns lead to more frequent and intense storms, causing floods, landslides, and the spread of waterborne diseases.

Presenter: Climate change also affects air quality, posing risks to respiratory health. Higher temperatures and changing weather patterns contribute to the formation of air pollutants, such as ground-level ozone and particulate matter. Exposure to these pollutants can worsen respiratory conditions such as asthma and lead to an increase in respiratory illnesses.

Presenter: Another area of concern is the spread of infectious diseases. Climate change, coupled with disruptions in ecosystems, can alter the distribution and behavior of disease-carrying organisms such as mosquitoes and ticks. This can lead to the spread of vector-borne diseases, including dengue fever, malaria, and Lyme disease, into new areas where populations may not have natural immunity.

Thank you for listening to today's lecture on the impact of climate change on global health. We hope you gained valuable insights into the connection between climate change and various health challenges faced worldwide.

Question 1:

What is the main topic of this lecture?

    A. The link between climate change and extreme weather events

    B. The impact of climate change on respiratory health

    C. The connection between climate change and infectious diseases

    D. The implications of climate change on global health

Explanation: The correct answer is d) The implications of climate change on global health. This question evaluates the test-taker's ability to comprehend and identify the main focus of the lecture. The presenter explicitly states that the lecture will explore the impact of climate change on global health.

Question 2:

What is one way in which climate change affects air quality, according to the lecture?

    A. Decreased formation of air pollutants

    B. Increased respiratory illnesses and conditions

    C. Stronger immune system response to pollutants

    D. Reduced risk of air pollution-related diseases

Explanation: The correct answer is b) Increased respiratory illnesses and conditions. This question measures the test-taker's comprehension skills. The presenter explains that climate change contributes to the formation of air pollutants, which can worsen respiratory conditions and lead to an increase in respiratory illnesses.

Question 3:

How does climate change contribute to the spread of vector-borne diseases?

    A. By decreasing the distribution of disease-carrying organisms

    B. By limiting the behavior of disease-carrying organisms

    C. By disrupting ecosystems and altering the distribution of disease-carrying organisms

    D. By reducing the risk of infectious diseases in new areas

Explanation: The correct answer is c) By disrupting ecosystems and altering the distribution of disease-carrying organisms. This question assesses the test-taker's comprehension skills. The presenter mentions that climate change, coupled with disruptions in ecosystems, can alter the distribution and behavior of disease-carrying organisms, leading to the spread of vector-borne diseases.

Question 4:

What is one impact of climate change on heat-related illnesses?

    A. Decreased severity and frequency of heatwaves

    B. Reduced risks of heat-related illnesses

    C. Increased occurrences and severity of heatwaves

    D. Improved ability to adapt and cope with heatwaves

Explanation: The correct answer is c) Increased occurrences and severity of heatwaves. This question evaluates the test-taker's comprehension skills. The presenter emphasizes that rising temperatures contribute to more frequent and severe heatwaves, which can result in heat-related illnesses and even death.

Question 5:

Based on the lecture, why is climate change a concern for global health?

    A. It promotes the spread of infectious diseases in everyday life

    B. It increases resistance to air pollutants and respiratory illnesses

    C. It enhances global efforts for disease prevention and control

    D. It poses risks to individuals and communities through various health challenges

Explanation: The correct answer is d) It poses risks to individuals and communities through various health challenges. This question assesses the test-taker's inference skills. Although not explicitly mentioned, the lecture emphasizes that climate change has far-reaching consequences for global health, including impacts on extreme weather events, air quality, and the spread of infectious diseases.

Practice Listening - 3

Title: The Impact of Artificial Intelligence on the Future Job Market Transcript

Presenter: Welcome, ladies and gentlemen. Today, we will discuss the impact of artificial intelligence (AI) on the future job market. AI, with its ability to automate tasks and analyze data at an unprecedented speed and scale, is revolutionizing industries and transforming the nature of work. In this lecture, we will explore both the potential benefits and challenges of AI on the job market. Let's delve into this important topic and examine how AI is shaping the future of work.

Presenter: One major benefit of AI in the job market is increased productivity and efficiency. AI technologies can automate routine and repetitive tasks, allowing workers to focus on more complex and creative endeavors. This not only improves productivity but also opens up new opportunities for innovation and growth.

Presenter: However, AI also presents challenges and potential risks. One concern is the displacement of certain job roles due to automation. Tasks that are mundane and predictable can be efficiently performed by AI systems, leading to decreased demand for human labor in those areas. This shift in the job market requires individuals to acquire new skills and adapt to changing work requirements.

Presenter: Additionally, the ethical implications of AI in the workforce need careful consideration. Issues such as bias in algorithms, privacy concerns, and the responsible use of AI-powered technologies highlight the importance of ethical guidelines and safeguards to protect workers and ensure fair and equitable practices.

Thank you for listening to today's lecture on the impact of artificial intelligence on the future job market. We hope you gained valuable insights into both the potential benefits and challenges of AI in the job market and how the future of work is being shaped.

Question 1:

What is the main topic of this lecture?

    A. The benefits of automation in the job market

    B. The impact of artificial intelligence on job roles

    C. The ethical considerations of artificial intelligence in the workforce

    D. The challenges and opportunities of artificial intelligence in the job market

Explanation: The correct answer is d) The challenges and opportunities of artificial intelligence in the job market. This question evaluates the test-taker's ability to comprehend and identify the main focus of the lecture. The presenter explicitly states that the lecture will explore both the potential benefits and challenges of AI on the job market.

Question 2:

What is one benefit of AI in the job market mentioned in the lecture?

    A. Increased demand for human labor

    B. Improved productivity and efficiency

    C. Decreased opportunities for innovation and growth

    D. Enhanced job security for workers

Explanation: The correct answer is b) Improved productivity and efficiency. This question measures the test-taker's comprehension skills. The presenter explains that AI technologies can automate routine tasks, leading to increased productivity and efficiency by allowing workers to focus on more complex and creative endeavors.

Question 3:

What is one potential challenge mentioned regarding AI in the job market?

    A. Increased demand for human labor in all areas

    B. Enhanced creativity and innovation among workers

    C. Displacement of certain job roles due to automation

    D. Indefinite job security and stability

Explanation: The correct answer is c) Displacement of certain job roles due to automation. This question assesses the test-taker's comprehension skills. The presenter mentions that AI can efficiently automate routine tasks, leading to decreased demand for human labor in certain areas, which can result in job role displacement.

Question 4:

What is one ethical consideration mentioned in the lecture regarding AI in the workforce?

    A. Decreased worker privacy and confidentiality

    B. Increased demand for AI-powered technologies

    C. Bias and fairness in AI algorithms

    D. Reduced need for ethical guidelines and safeguards

Explanation: The correct answer is c) Bias and fairness in AI algorithms. This question evaluates the test-taker's comprehension skills. The presenter highlights the importance of considering issues such as bias in algorithms as an ethical consideration in the use of AI-powered technologies in the workforce.

Question 5:

Based on the lecture, what is the overall impact of AI on the job market?

    A. Decreased productivity and innovation

    B. Unemployment and job insecurity for workers

    C. Displacement of certain job roles and the need for new skills

    D. Increased demand for routine and repetitive tasks

Explanation: The correct answer is c) Displacement of certain job roles and the need for new skills. This question assesses the test-taker's inference skills. Although not explicitly mentioned, the lecture emphasizes that AI automation may lead to the displacement of certain job roles, requiring individuals to acquire new skills and adapt to changing work requirements.

Practice Listening - 4

Title: The Impact of Social Media on Youth Mental Health Transcript

Lecturer: Good afternoon, class. Today, we will be examining the impact of social media on youth mental health. With the increasing use of social media platforms among young individuals, it is crucial to understand the potential effects they may have on mental well-being. In this lecture, we will explore both the positive and negative aspects of social media and its implications for youth mental health. Let's delve into this topic and uncover the influence of social media on young minds.

Lecturer: Firstly, let's explore the positive aspects. Social media can provide a sense of connection and enable individuals to maintain relationships and connect with friends from various locations. It can help create virtual communities and foster support for those facing similar challenges. Moreover, social media can serve as a platform for self-expression and creativity, allowing young people to share their thoughts, talents, and receive validation from their peers.

Lecturer: On the other hand, the excessive use of social media can have detrimental effects on youth mental health. One of the negative aspects is the potential for cyberbullying. Online harassment, spreading rumors, or posting hurtful comments can profoundly impact the mental well-being of young individuals, leading to anxiety, depression, or even suicidal thoughts.

Furthermore, constantly comparing oneself to others' highlight reels on social media platforms can create feelings of inadequacy, low self-esteem, and a distorted perception of reality.

Lecturer: It is important for young people to be aware of the potential risks and unhealthy habits associated with social media use. Developing healthy online habits, setting boundaries, and seeking support from trusted adults or mental health professionals can mitigate the negative impact of social media on youth mental health.

Now, let's move on to some questions to assess your comprehension and inference skills.

Question 1:

What is the main focus of this lecture?

    A. The positive impact of social media on mental health

    B. The negative impact of social media on mental health

    C. The relationship between youth and social media

    D. The benefits and drawbacks of youth mental health

Correct answer: c) The relationship between youth and social media.

Explanation: The lecture examines the impact of social media specifically on youth mental health, highlighting the importance of understanding this relationship.

Question 2:

What is one positive aspect of social media mentioned in the lecture?

    A. Increased risk of cyberbullying

    B. Formation of virtual communities

    C. Negative impact on creativity

    D. Distorted perception of reality

Correct answer: b) Formation of virtual communities.

Explanation: The lecturer mentions that social media can create virtual communities and foster support for individuals facing similar challenges.

Question 3:

What is one potential negative impact of excessive social media use discussed in the lecture?

    A. Increased self-esteem and validation from peers

    B. Distorted perception of reality

    C. Enhancement of creativity and self-expression

    D. Potential for cyberbullying and mental health issues

Correct answer: d) Potential for cyberbullying and mental health issues.

Explanation: The lecturer explains that excessive social media use can lead to cyberbullying, which can have a profound impact on the mental well-being of young individuals.

Question 4:

What action can mitigate the negative impact of social media on youth mental health?

    A. Developing unhealthy online habits

    B. Setting no boundaries for social media use

    C. Seeking support from mental health professionals

    D. Constant comparison to others on social media

Correct answer: c) Seeking support from mental health professionals.

Explanation: The lecturer recommends seeking support from trusted adults or mental health professionals as a way to mitigate the negative impact of social media on youth mental health.

Question 5:

What is one potential positive impact of social media use according to the lecture?

    A. Increased risk of depressive thoughts and low self-esteem

    B. Enhanced self-expression and creative outlets

    C. Limited connectivity and sense of isolation

    D. Negative reinforcement and validation-seeking behavior

Correct answer: b) Enhanced self-expression and creative outlets.

Explanation: The lecturer mentions that social media can serve as a platform for self-expression and creativity, allowing young people to share their thoughts and talents.

Practice Listening - 5

Title: The Advantages and Disadvantages of Online Learning Transcript

Presenter: Good morning, everyone. Today, we will explore the advantages and disadvantages of online learning. In recent years, online education has gained popularity due to its flexibility and accessibility. However, it is essential to consider both the benefits and drawbacks of this mode of learning. In this lecture, we will delve into the advantages and disadvantages of online learning and discuss its implications for students. Let's proceed and uncover the pros and cons of online education.

Presenter: One of the significant advantages of online learning is flexibility. Students have the freedom to access course materials at their own pace and convenience, allowing for personalized learning experiences. This flexibility is particularly beneficial for individuals with other commitments or those who prefer a self-paced learning environment.

Presenter: Another advantage is the access to a wide range of resources. Online platforms provide students with an abundance of materials, including multimedia resources, interactive activities, and diverse perspectives. This enables learners to engage with a variety of resources beyond traditional textbooks, fostering a more enriching educational experience.

Presenter: However, online learning also comes with certain disadvantages. One major drawback is the lack of face-to-face interaction. Without physical classrooms, students may miss out on direct interaction with peers and instructors, which can limit collaborative learning and immediate feedback.

Presenter: Additionally, online learning requires self-discipline and motivation. Students need to be proactive in managing their time, staying organized, and actively participating in the virtual learning environment. For some individuals, the absence of a structured setting and external accountability can present challenges.

Thank you for listening to today's lecture on the advantages and disadvantages of online learning. We hope you gained valuable insights into the flexibility and benefits of online education, as well as the challenges and considerations to keep in mind.

Question 1:

What is the main topic of this lecture?

    A. The advantages of traditional classroom learning

    B. The drawbacks of online education

    C. The benefits and challenges of online learning

    D. The importance of self-discipline in education

Explanation: The correct answer is c) The benefits and challenges of online learning. This question evaluates the test-taker's ability to comprehend and identify the main focus of the lecture. The presenter explicitly states that the lecture will explore both the advantages and disadvantages of online learning.

Question 2:

What is one advantage of online learning mentioned in the lecture?

    A. Limited access to educational resources

    B. Restricted flexibility and pacing

    C. Personalized learning experiences and flexibility

    D. Direct interaction with peers and instructors

Explanation: The correct answer is c) Personalized learning experiences and flexibility. This question measures the test-taker's comprehension skills. The presenter mentions that online learning offers flexibility and personalized learning experiences, allowing students to access course materials at their own pace and convenience.

Question 3:

What is one disadvantage of online learning discussed in the lecture?

    A. Limited access to learning resources

    B. Increased face-to-face interaction

    C. Lack of collaboration and immediate feedback

    D. Enhanced self-discipline and motivation

Explanation: The correct answer is c) Lack of collaboration and immediate feedback. This question assesses the test-taker's comprehension skills. The presenter explains that without physical classrooms, students may miss out on direct interaction with peers and instructors, limiting collaborative learning and immediate feedback.

Question 4:

What skill or characteristic is necessary for successful online learning, as mentioned in the lecture?

    A. External accountability and structured setting

    B. Passive participation and time management

    C. Motivation and self-discipline

    D. Procrastination and disorganization

Explanation: The correct answer is c) Motivation and self-discipline. This question measures the test-taker's comprehension skills. The presenter highlights that online learning requires self-discipline and motivation, as students need to manage their time, stay organized, and actively participate in the virtual learning environment.

Question 5:

Based on the lecture, what is one potential advantage of online learning?

    A. Limited access to resources beyond traditional textbooks

    B. Decreased flexibility and personalized learning experiences

    C. Enhanced face-to-face interaction and immediate feedback

    D. Access to a wide range of multimedia resources and perspectives

Explanation: The correct answer is d) Access to a wide range of multimedia resources and perspectives. This question assesses the test-taker's inference skills. Although not explicitly mentioned, the presenter discusses the advantage of online learning being the access to diverse resources, including multimedia materials, interactive activities, and diverse perspectives.

Practice Listening - 6

Title: The Impact of Deforestation on Climate Change
Transcript

Presenter: Welcome, ladies and gentlemen. Today, we will discuss the critical issue of deforestation and its impact on climate change. Deforestation, the clearing of forests by human activities, has severe consequences for both the environment and the global climate. In this lecture, we will explore the relationship between deforestation and climate change and the importance of finding sustainable solutions. Let's dive into this pressing topic and uncover the implications of deforestation.

Presenter: Deforestation contributes to climate change in several ways. First, trees play a crucial role in regulating the Earth's temperature by absorbing carbon dioxide, a greenhouse gas, through photosynthesis. When forests are cleared, this natural carbon sink diminishes, resulting in increased greenhouse gas emissions and the intensification of global warming.

Presenter: Secondly, deforestation disrupts the water cycle, leading to altered rainfall patterns and droughts. Forests act as essential water catchment areas, capturing moisture and releasing it gradually. Without forests, rainfall becomes unpredictable, affecting agriculture, freshwater availability, and overall ecosystem stability.

Presenter: Lastly, deforestation contributes to the loss of biodiversity. Forests are home to an incredible diversity of plant and animal species, providing critical habitats. The destruction of these habitats due to deforestation not only threatens the survival of countless species but also disrupts the delicate balance of ecosystems.

Thank you for listening to today's lecture on the impact of deforestation on climate change. We hope you gained valuable insights into the consequences of deforestation and the significance of finding sustainable solutions to this crucial issue.

Question 1:
What is the main topic of this lecture?

      A. The importance of forest conservation

B. The consequences of deforestation on climate change

   C. The role of greenhouse gases in global warming

   D. The correlation between deforestation and natural disasters

Explanation: The correct answer is b) The consequences of deforestation on climate change. This question evaluates the test-taker's ability to comprehend and identify the main subject of the lecture. The presenter explicitly states that the lecture focuses on the impact of deforestation on climate change.

Question 2:

How does deforestation contribute to increased greenhouse gas emissions?

   A. By reducing the carbon dioxide absorption of trees

   B. By promoting the growth of greenhouse gas-emitting industries

   C. By enhancing the natural carbon sink

   D. By increasing the rate of photosynthesis

Explanation: The correct answer is a) By reducing the carbon dioxide absorption of the trees. This question measures the test-taker's comprehension skills. The presenter explains that deforestation diminishes the natural carbon sink, resulting in increased greenhouse gas emissions.

Question 3:

What is one consequence of deforestation mentioned in the lecture?

   A. Improved ecosystem stability

   B. Increased water availability and predictable rainfall

   C. Enhanced agricultural productivity

   D. Disruption of the water cycle and altered rainfall patterns

Explanation: The correct answer is d) Disruption of the water cycle and altered rainfall patterns. This question assesses the test-taker's comprehension skills. The presenter highlights that deforestation disrupts the water cycle, leading to altered rainfall patterns and potential droughts.

Question 4:

According to the lecture, what is one impact of deforestation on biodiversity?

    A. Conservation of critical habitats

    B. Promotion of species diversity

    C. Disruption of ecosystems and species loss

    D. Enhanced resilience of plant and animal species

Explanation: The correct answer is c) Disruption of ecosystems and species loss. This question evaluates the test-taker's comprehension skills. The presenter explains that deforestation threatens biodiversity by disrupting ecosystems and potentially leading to the loss of species.

Question 5:

Based on the lecture, why is it crucial to find sustainable solutions to deforestation?

    A. To promote industrial development and economic growth

    B. To improve timber and wood industry practices

    C. To mitigate the impacts of climate change

    D. To encourage the expansion of agricultural activities

Explanation: The correct answer is c) To mitigate the impacts of climate change. This question assesses the test-taker's inference skills. Although not explicitly mentioned, the lecture emphasizes that finding sustainable solutions to deforestation is critical in addressing climate change, which suggests the importance of mitigating its impacts.

Practice Listening - 7

Title: The Importance of Renewable Energy Transcript

Presenter: Welcome, everyone. Today, we will explore the importance of renewable energy in combating climate change and transitioning towards a sustainable future. Renewable energy sources, such as solar, wind, and hydroelectric power, offer numerous benefits for environmental, economic, and social well-being. In this lecture, we will delve into the advantages of renewable energy and its role in addressing global energy needs. Let's proceed and uncover the significance of embracing renewable energy.

Presenter: Renewable energy sources are crucial in combatting climate change. Unlike fossil fuels, which release greenhouse gases when burned, renewable energy technologies produce little to no emissions, reducing carbon footprints. Harnessing the power of the sun, wind, and water helps mitigate the impacts of climate change and contributes to a cleaner, healthier environment.

Presenter: A significant advantage of renewable energy is its potential for job creation and economic growth. Investments in renewable energy infrastructure lead to the establishment of new industries and the development of green jobs. By transitioning to renewable energy sources, societies can stimulate local economies, enhance energy security, and reduce dependence on fossil fuel imports.

Presenter: Another benefit of renewable energy is its accessibility and potential for energy equity. In many regions, renewable resources are abundant and can provide decentralized energy solutions. This enables communities, particularly those in remote areas, to access affordable and reliable electricity, improving their quality of life.

Thank you for listening to today's lecture on the importance of renewable energy. We hope you gained valuable insights into the advantages and significance of renewable energy sources in addressing global challenges and achieving a sustainable energy future.

Question 1:

What is the main topic of this lecture?

    A. The advantages of renewable energy sources

    B. The challenges of transitioning to renewable energy

    C. The economic benefits of fossil fuel industries

    D. The correlation between renewable energy and climate change

Explanation: The correct answer is a) The advantages of renewable energy sources. This question measures the test-taker's ability to comprehend and identify the main focus of the lecture. The presenter explicitly states that the lecture will explore the benefits of renewable energy.

Question 2:

What is one advantage of renewable energy mentioned in the lecture?

    A. Increased emissions and air pollution

    B. Job creation and economic growth

    C. Dependence on fossil fuel imports

    D. Limited accessibility to energy resources

Explanation: The correct answer is b) Job creation and economic growth. This question assesses the test-taker's comprehension skills. The presenter highlights that investments in renewable energy lead to the establishment of new industries and the creation of green jobs.

Question 3:

How does renewable energy contribute to combating climate change?

    A. By emitting more greenhouse gases than fossil fuels

    B. By reducing carbon footprints and emissions

    C. By increasing dependence on fossil fuel imports

    D. By aggravating the impacts of climate change

Explanation: The correct answer is b) By reducing carbon footprints and emissions. This question measures the test-taker's comprehension skills. The presenter explains that renewable energy technologies produce little to no emissions, contributing to a cleaner environment and mitigating the impacts of climate change.

Question 4:

According to the lecture, what is one potential benefit of renewable energy for communities?

    A. Enhanced energy security and independence

    B. Increased reliance on fossil fuel imports

    C. Limited access to affordable electricity

    D. Higher costs of energy production

Explanation: The correct answer is a) Enhanced energy security and independence. This question evaluates the test-taker's comprehension skills. The presenter emphasizes that renewable energy sources provide decentralized energy solutions, enabling communities to access affordable and reliable electricity, thereby enhancing energy security and independence.

Question 5:

Based on the lecture, why is embracing renewable energy significant?

    A. To promote job creation in fossil fuel industries

    B. To increase dependence on imported energy resources

    C. To accelerate climate change and its impacts

    D. To transition towards a cleaner, more sustainable future

Explanation: The correct answer is d) To transition towards a cleaner, more sustainable future. This question assesses the test-taker's inference skills. Although not explicitly mentioned, the lecture emphasizes that embracing renewable energy is important in combating climate change and transitioning towards a more sustainable future.

Practice Listening - 8

Title: The Benefits of Cultural Diversity Transcript

Presenter: Welcome, ladies and gentlemen. Today, we will explore the value and benefits of cultural diversity. Every society is enriched by its diverse cultures, traditions, and perspectives. In this lecture, we will discuss how cultural diversity contributes to social, economic, and intellectual growth. Let's dive into the significance of embracing and celebrating diversity in our communities.

Presenter: Cultural diversity promotes social cohesion and inclusion. By embracing and accepting different cultures, we foster a sense of belonging for all individuals within society. This inclusivity not only strengthens social bonds but also encourages mutual respect and understanding among diverse communities.

Presenter: Economic benefits also arise from cultural diversity. Exchanges of ideas, practices, and products between cultures stimulate innovation and economic growth. Businesses that embrace diversity and foster an inclusive environment tend to attract diverse talent and tap into new markets, leading to greater success and competitiveness.

Presenter: Intellectual growth is another significant outcome of cultural diversity. Exposure to different perspectives and worldviews broadens one's understanding and challenges existing assumptions. Interacting with individuals from diverse backgrounds and cultures promotes critical thinking, creativity, and cross-cultural competency.

Thank you for listening to today's lecture on the benefits of cultural diversity. We hope you gained valuable insights into the importance of embracing diversity and celebrating the richness that different cultures bring to our societies.

Question 1:

What is the main topic of this lecture?

    A. The challenges of cultural diversity in society

    B. The economic impact of cultural exchange

    C. The benefits of embracing cultural diversity

D. The role of cultural traditions in modern societies

Explanation: The correct answer is c) The benefits of embracing cultural diversity. This question evaluates the test-taker's ability to comprehend and identify the main focus of the lecture. The presenter explicitly states that the lecture will discuss the value and benefits of cultural diversity.

Question 2:

What is one benefit of cultural diversity mentioned in the lecture?

A. Increased social isolation and exclusion

B. Reduced economic growth and innovation

C. Strengthened social bonds and inclusivity

D. Limited exposure to new ideas and perspectives

Explanation: The correct answer is c) Strengthened social bonds and inclusivity. This question assesses the test-taker's comprehension skills. The presenter explains that cultural diversity promotes social cohesion and inclusivity, fostering a sense of belonging and strengthening social bonds.

Question 3:

According to the lecture, how does cultural diversity contribute to economic growth?

A. By limiting access to diverse talent and new markets

B. By discouraging innovation and entrepreneurship

C. By attracting diverse talent and tapping into new markets

D. By hindering intercultural communication and collaboration

Explanation: The correct answer is c) By attracting diverse talent and tapping into new markets. This question measures the test-taker's comprehension skills. The presenter mentions that businesses that embrace diversity tend to attract diverse talent and tap into new markets, leading to greater success and competitiveness.

Question 4:

What is one impact of cultural diversity on intellectual growth?

A. Narrowed understanding and limited perspectives

B. Decreased critical thinking and creativity

C. Restriction of cross-cultural competency

D. Broadened understanding and increased creativity

Explanation: The correct answer is d) Broadened understanding and increased creativity. This question evaluates the test-taker's comprehension skills. The presenter explains that exposure to diverse perspectives promotes critical thinking, creativity, and cross-cultural competency.

Question 5:

Based on the lecture, why is embracing cultural diversity significant?

    A. To promote social isolation and exclusion

    B. To limit economic growth and innovation

    C. To encourage cultural assimilation and uniformity

    D. To foster social cohesion, economic growth, and intellectual development

Explanation: The correct answer is d) To foster social cohesion, economic growth, and intellectual development. This question assesses the test-taker's inference skills. Although not explicitly mentioned, the lecture emphasizes the significance of embracing cultural diversity for social cohesion, economic benefits, and intellectual growth.

Practice Listening - 9

Title: The Importance of Early Childhood Education
Transcript

Presenter: Good morning, everyone. Today, we will discuss the crucial role of early childhood education in shaping the development and future success of children. Early childhood education encompasses the period from birth to age eight and provides a strong foundation for lifelong learning. In this lecture, we will explore the benefits of early childhood education and its impact on cognitive, social, and emotional growth. Let's dive into this important topic and understand the significance of investing in early education.

Presenter: Early childhood education plays a vital role in cognitive development. During these formative years, children's brains are rapidly developing, and quality early education experiences stimulate their cognitive abilities, including language proficiency, problem-solving skills, and memory retention. This foundation enhances academic performance and lays the groundwork for future learning.

Presenter: Social and emotional development is another critical aspect addressed in early childhood education. Interaction with peers and skilled educators fosters the development of social skills, cooperation, empathy, and emotional regulation. A positive early learning experience creates a nurturing environment where children feel supported, building their self- esteem and sense of belonging.

Presenter: Early childhood education also contributes to reduced inequality. Providing access to quality education during these early years helps bridge the gap between advantaged and disadvantaged children, setting them on a more equitable path. It prepares them for future educational opportunities, narrowing the achievement gap and promoting social mobility.

Thank you for listening to today's lecture on the importance of early childhood education. We hope you gained valuable insights into the benefits of early education in shaping children's cognitive, social, and emotional growth.

Question 1:

What is the main topic of this lecture?

    A. The benefits of quality education

    B. The development of cognitive skills

    C. The importance of early childhood education

    D. The role of educators in shaping children's minds

Explanation: The correct answer is c) The importance of early childhood education. This question measures the test-taker's ability to comprehend and identify the main focus of the lecture. The presenter explicitly states that the lecture will discuss the crucial role of early childhood education.

Question 2:

What aspect of development does early childhood education primarily focus on?

    A. Emotional regulation and empathy

    B. Physical growth and motor skills

    C. Language proficiency and problem-solving

    D. Adolescence and self-identity

Explanation: The correct answer is c) Language proficiency and problem-solving. This question assesses the test-taker's comprehension skills. The presenter mentions that early childhood education stimulates cognitive abilities, including language proficiency and problem-solving skills, during the rapidly developing years.

Question 3:

How does early childhood education contribute to the development of social skills?

    A. By promoting cooperation and empathy

    B. By encouraging physical growth and fitness

    C. By emphasizing competitive behavior

    D. By prioritizing individual achievement

Explanation: The correct answer is a) By promoting cooperation and empathy. This question measures the test-taker's comprehension skills. The presenter explains that early childhood education fosters the development of social skills, including cooperation and empathy, through interaction with peers and educators.

Question 4:

What is one potential benefit of early childhood education mentioned in the lecture?

    A. Enhanced cognitive abilities and academic performance

    B. Limited access to educational opportunities

    C. Wider inequality between advantaged and disadvantaged children

    D. Increased competition and stress among students

Explanation: The correct answer is a) Enhanced cognitive abilities and academic performance. This question evaluates the test-taker's comprehension skills. The presenter highlights that quality early education experiences stimulate cognitive abilities and enhance academic performance.

Question 5:

Based on the lecture, why is investing in early childhood education significant?

    A. To promote competition and individual achievement

    B. To exacerbate inequality and social divisions

    C. To build the foundation for lifelong learning and success

    D. To limit access to educational opportunities

Explanation: The correct answer is c) To build the foundation for lifelong learning and success. This question assesses the test-taker's inference skills. Although not explicitly stated, the lecture emphasizes that investing in early childhood education is crucial in establishing a strong foundation for future learning and success.

Practice Listening - 10

Title: The Impact of Climate Change on Global Agriculture Transcript

Presenter: Good morning, everyone. Today, we will discuss the impact of climate change on global agriculture. Climate change is significantly altering weather patterns, temperatures, and precipitation levels, leading to various challenges for farmers worldwide. In this lecture, we will explore how climate change affects crop production, food security, and agricultural practices. Let's delve into this critical topic and understand the implications for global food systems.

Presenter: One major impact of climate change on agriculture is altered growing conditions. Rising temperatures and changing rainfall patterns can disrupt traditional growing seasons and affect crop yields. For example, prolonged droughts in certain regions can lead to water scarcity and crop failures, while increased temperatures may accelerate the growth of pests and diseases, posing further challenges for farmers.

Presenter: Another consequence is the loss of arable land due to factors such as desertification, soil erosion, and sea-level rise. As temperatures rise and extreme weather events become more frequent, agricultural land becomes degraded or submerged, reducing the available land for cultivation. This loss of arable land threatens food production and exacerbates food insecurity in vulnerable regions.

Presenter: Furthermore, climate change impacts agricultural biodiversity and ecosystems. Shifts in temperature and precipitation patterns can disrupt natural habitats and migration patterns of pollinators and beneficial insects essential for crop pollination and pest control. This disruption can lead to decreased crop yields and increased reliance on synthetic inputs, further straining agricultural sustainability.

Thank you for listening to today's lecture on the impact of climate change on global agriculture. We hope you gained valuable insights into the challenges facing farmers and food systems worldwide.

Question 1:

What is the main topic of this lecture?

    A. The benefits of organic farming

    B. The impact of climate change on global agriculture

    C. Strategies for improving crop yields

    D. The role of technology in modern farming practices

Explanation: The correct answer is b) The impact of climate change on global agriculture. This question measures the test-taker's ability to comprehend and identify the main focus of the lecture. The presenter explicitly states that the lecture will discuss how climate change affects crop production, food security, and agricultural practices.

Question 2:

What is one consequence of climate change mentioned in the lecture regarding agriculture?

    A. Decreased use of synthetic inputs in farming

    B. Increased availability of arable land for cultivation

    C. Loss of arable land due to desertification and soil erosion

    D. Expansion of natural habitats for pollinators

Explanation: The correct answer is c) Loss of arable land due to desertification and soil erosion. This question assesses the test-taker's comprehension skills. The presenter mentions that climate change can lead to factors such as desertification, soil erosion, and sea-level rise, resulting in the loss of arable land.

Question 3:

How can climate change impact agricultural biodiversity?

    A. By promoting the migration of pollinators and beneficial insects

    B. By decreasing reliance on synthetic inputs in farming

    C. By enhancing natural habitats for wildlife

    D. By disrupting migration patterns of pollinators and beneficial insects

Explanation: The correct answer is d) By disrupting migration patterns of pollinators and beneficial insects. This question measures the test-taker's comprehension skills. The presenter explains that shifts in temperature and precipitation patterns can disrupt natural habitats and migration patterns of pollinators and beneficial insects, impacting agricultural biodiversity.

Question 4:

What is one challenge mentioned in the lecture regarding altered growing conditions due to climate change?

    A. Increased water availability leading to enhanced crop yields

    B. Accelerated growth of pests and diseases

    C. Reduced reliance on irrigation systems

    D. Longer growing seasons resulting in increased crop diversity

Explanation: The correct answer is b) Accelerated growth of pests and diseases. This question evaluates the test-taker's comprehension skills. The presenter mentions that increased temperatures may accelerate the growth of pests and diseases, posing challenges for farmers due to altered growing conditions.

Question 5:

Based on the lecture, why is climate change a significant concern for global agriculture?

    A. To promote the expansion of agricultural biodiversity

    B. To increase the availability of arable land for cultivation

    C. To enhance food security and crop yields

    D. To reduce reliance on synthetic inputs in farming

Explanation: The correct answer is c) To enhance food security and crop yields. This question assesses the test-taker's inference skills. Although not explicitly stated, the lecture emphasizes that climate change poses challenges such as altered growing conditions, loss of arable land, and impacts on agricultural biodiversity, which collectively threaten food security and crop yields on a global scale.

Speaking Section

How to master the speaking section?

The speaking section of the TOEFL exam evaluates a test-taker's ability to communicate effectively in English. It comprises four tasks that assess different aspects of spoken English proficiency. To excel in this section, it is crucial to understand its structure and implement effective preparation strategies.

The TOEFL speaking section consists of the following tasks:

Task 1 - Independent Speaking: In this task, test-takers express their opinions on familiar topics. They have 15 seconds to prepare and 45 seconds to respond. Topics can range from personal experiences to general issues.

Task 2 - Integrated Speaking: This task assesses the ability to integrate information from both listening and reading passages. Test-takers have 30 seconds to prepare and 60 seconds to speak. They must synthesize the provided information and express their opinion or provide a summary.

Task 3 - Integrated Speaking: Similar to Task 2, this task requires test-takers to integrate information from listening and reading materials. However, they have to summarize a conversation or lecture. The preparation time is 20 seconds, and the speaking time is 60 seconds.

Task 4 - Integrated Speaking: In this task, test-takers listen to a lecture and respond to it. They have 30 seconds to prepare and 60 seconds to answer. The response should demonstrate comprehension and express a clear and organized opinion.

To master the speaking section, consider the following strategies:

Build vocabulary and practice pronunciation: Enhance your vocabulary by studying and using diverse words and phrases. Practice pronunciation and intonation to ensure clarity in your speech.

Develop effective time management: Efficiently manage the preparation time for each task. Practice organizing your thoughts quickly to deliver a coherent response within the given time limit.

Utilize templates and structures: Familiarize yourself with common speaking templates and structures to organize your responses effectively. This will help you convey your ideas in a clear and organized manner.

Focus on fluency and coherence: Aim for a smooth and natural flow of speech. Use appropriate transition words and linking phrases to create coherence between ideas. Maintain a steady pace and avoid prolonged pauses or hesitations.

Practice active listening and note-taking: Enhance your listening skills and note-taking abilities. During integrated tasks, take efficient notes to capture key points and details for reference while formulating your response.

Seek feedback and practice speaking tasks: Practice speaking tasks similar to those found in the TOEFL exam. Seek feedback from teachers, tutors, or language exchange partners to refine your spoken English skills.

Familiarize yourself with different accents: Expose yourself to a variety of English accents by listening to podcasts, lectures, or interviews. This will help you understand different speech patterns and enhance your listening comprehension.

By understanding the structure of the speaking section and implementing these strategies, you can effectively prepare for the TOEFL speaking section and increase your chances of success. Regular practice, focused preparation, and confidence in your abilities will contribute to your overall performance in this section.

Speaking Task 1 Example - Opinion

Some people believe that technology has brought more harm than good to society. Do you agree or disagree? Provide specific examples and reasons to support your opinion.

Sample Excellent Response:

In my opinion, I disagree that technology has brought more harm than good to society. While there are certainly negative aspects associated with technology, its overall impact has been overwhelmingly positive. Firstly, technology has improved communication by enabling people to connect easily across long distances. Platforms like social media have allowed individuals to maintain relationships and share important information effortlessly. Secondly, technology has revolutionized various industries, leading to advancements in healthcare, transportation, and education. For instance, medical technologies have enhanced diagnosis and treatment, making healthcare more efficient and accessible. Similarly, online learning platforms have expanded educational opportunities for people worldwide. Lastly, technology has contributed to economic growth by creating new job opportunities and streamlining business operations. Companies have achieved remarkable productivity with the aid of automation and digital tools. Hence, while technology has its challenges, its positive influence on society cannot be overlooked.

Tips for Test Takers: To effectively respond to this prompt, consider the following tips:

1. **Clearly state your opinion:** Begin your response by clearly indicating whether you agree or disagree with the prompt statement. This sets the tone for your overall response.

2. **Provide specific examples:** Support your opinion with specific examples and relevant details. This helps to strengthen your arguments and demonstrate a deep understanding of the topic.

3. **Develop a well-structured response:** Organize your thoughts with an introduction, body paragraphs, and a conclusion. Each paragraph should focus on a distinct point or example, and use transition words to ensure a smooth flow of thoughts.

4. **Speak confidently and fluently:** Practice beforehand to improve your speaking fluency and confidence. Maintain a steady pace, use appropriate intonation, and vary your vocabulary to express your ideas effectively.

5. **Use connecting words and phrases:** Employ connecting words and phrases (e.g., Firstly, Secondly, Lastly) to provide a clear structure to your response. This showcases your ability to organize information logically.

6. **Consider counterarguments:** While not necessary, you may choose to briefly mention counterarguments to further validate your position. This demonstrates a balanced perspective and critical thinking skills.

7. **Time management:** Keep track of time during your preparation and response. Allocate sufficient time to brainstorm ideas, structure your response, and provide specific examples within the given time limit.

Speaking Task 2
Example - Conversation

Analytical TOEFL-style Speaking Question: Listen to a complex conversation between two experts discussing the ethical implications of genetic engineering. Based on the conversation, discuss the potential benefits and concerns associated with the use of genetic engineering in agriculture. Use specific examples and arguments from the conversation to support your response.

[Transcript]

Speaker 1: Good afternoon, Dr. Smith. I wanted to discuss the ethical implications of genetic engineering in agriculture with you. It's a complex topic that's been receiving a lot of attention lately.

Speaker 2: Yes, it is indeed a complex issue, and an important one to consider. Genetic engineering has the potential to revolutionize agriculture, but it also raises significant concerns. Let's examine both sides.

Speaker 1: Absolutely. One of the benefits of genetic engineering in agriculture is the ability to create crops that are resistant to pests and diseases. By introducing specific genes into the plants, we can reduce the need for pesticides and, in turn, minimize the environmental impact.

Speaker 2: That's true. Genetic modification can enhance crop productivity and increase yields, contributing to food security. We have the potential to develop crops that are more resilient to harsh environmental conditions, allowing us to grow food even in challenging climates.

Speaker 1: Agreed. Another benefit is the capacity to improve the nutritional content of crops. Genetic engineering can be used to enhance vitamin content or reduce allergenic properties in certain foods, which can have significant health benefits for the population.

Speaker 2: However, we must also address the concerns associated with genetic engineering in agriculture. One major concern is the potential for unintended ecological consequences.

Genetically modified crops may interact with the environment in unforeseen ways, leading to the emergence of "superweeds" or harm to non-target organisms.

Speaker 1: Yes, that's a valid point. Thorough risk assessment is crucial to mitigate these risks. We need to conduct comprehensive studies and closely monitor the long-term effects of genetic modification on ecosystems.

Speaker 2: Another concern is the socio-economic impact of genetic engineering in agriculture. The patenting of genetically modified seeds and the associated intellectual property rights can lead to the commercialization and monopolization of the agricultural industry. This may disadvantage small farmers and negatively impact the diversity of our food system.

Speaker 1: Absolutely. We need to ensure that access to genetically modified crops and technologies is not limited to a few large corporations. It should be accessible to all, particularly small-scale farmers who play an important role in sustainable agriculture.

Speaker 2: Lastly, we cannot overlook the ethical implications of tinkering with the genetic makeup of organisms. Some argue that we are venturing into unknown territory and that tampering with nature in this way goes against our moral responsibilities.

Speaker 1: Agreed. Ethical considerations are of utmost importance when it comes to

genetic engineering. We need to balance our desire for innovation and progress with the potential risks and unintended consequences that may arise.

Speaker 2: Indeed, it's a delicate balance. Robust regulations, transparency, and stakeholder involvement are essential to ensure responsible and ethical practices in genetic engineering.

Speaker 1: I couldn't agree more. Striking that balance is crucial as we move forward in harnessing the potential of genetic engineering in agriculture.

Speaker 2: Absolutely. It's a topic that requires ongoing dialogue and careful consideration. The decisions we make today will have a long-lasting impact on the future of our food system and the environment.

Speaker 1: Thank you for the insightful discussion, Dr. Smith. It's always a pleasure to exchange ideas with you.

Speaker 2: Likewise. Thank you for initiating this conversation. Let's continue to explore these complex issues and work towards a sustainable and ethical approach to genetic engineering in agriculture.

[End of transcript]

Sample Excellent Response:

According to the conversation, the use of genetic engineering in agriculture presents both potential benefits and concerns. One major benefit highlighted in the discussion is the ability to create genetically modified crops that are resistant to pests and diseases, thereby reducing the need for pesticides and increasing crop yields. The experts mention that this can contribute to food security by ensuring a stable and abundant food supply. Additionally, genetic engineering allows for the enhancement of nutritional value in crops, such as increasing vitamin content or reducing allergenic properties, which can positively impact public health.

However, the conversation also highlights several concerns associated with the use of genetic engineering in agriculture. One concern raised is the potential ecological impact of genetically modified crops. The experts discuss the possibility of unintended ecological consequences, such as the creation of "superweeds" or the harm to non-target organisms due to genetically modified traits. These concerns underscore the need for thorough risk assessment and mitigation strategies to minimize potential negative effects.

Furthermore, the conversation addresses the issue of socio-economic implications. The experts discuss how the patenting of genetically modified seeds and associated intellectual property rights can lead to commercialization and monopolization of the agricultural industry, potentially disadvantaging small farmers and creating dependency on seed corporations. They also touch upon ethical concerns about the long-term implications of tinkering with the genetic makeup of organisms.

In conclusion, the conversation presents a nuanced perspective on the benefits and concerns of using genetic engineering in agriculture. While genetic modification can enhance crop productivity, improve nutritional value, and contribute to food security, it also raises ecological, socio-economic, and ethical concerns. Striking a balance between harnessing the potential benefits and mitigating the associated risks requires robust regulations, transparency, and stakeholder engagement.

Strategies for Test-Takers:

1. **Active listening and note-taking:** Focus on key points and arguments discussed in the conversation. Take concise notes to ensure accuracy and facilitate a well-structured response.

2. **Address all aspects of the question:** Provide a comprehensive response by discussing both the potential benefits and concerns associated with the use of genetic engineering in agriculture, using specific examples and arguments from the conversation.

3. **Organize your response:** Structure your response with an introduction, body paragraphs, and a conclusion. Clearly present each point or argument and maintain a logical flow throughout your response.

4. **Develop and support your arguments:** Use examples, evidence, and reasoning from the conversation to strengthen your arguments. Elaborate on the specific benefits and concerns mentioned by the experts to demonstrate an understanding of the topic.

5. **Use appropriate language and vocabulary:** Employ a range of vocabulary and sentence structures to express your ideas effectively. Use appropriate transition words to enhance the coherence and cohesion of your response.

6. **Time management:** Practice effective time management during your preparation and response. Allocate sufficient time to brainstorm ideas, organize your thoughts, and deliver a well-rounded response within the given time limit.

7. **Practice critical thinking:** Engage with the complex issues discussed in the conversation and demonstrate critical thinking skills by considering multiple perspectives and implications. This will help you provide a balanced and thoughtful response.

Remember to practice actively listening to complex conversations, summarize key points, and respond fluently. Regular practice will enhance your listening comprehension and speaking skills, enabling you to excel in the TOEFL-speaking section.

Speaking Task 3 Example - Academic Lecture

Analytical TOEFL-style Speaking Question: Listen to a complex physics lecture discussing the theory of relativity. Based on the lecture, explain the concept of time dilation and its implications for space travel. Use specific examples and arguments from the lecture to support your response.

[Transcript]

Speaker: Good afternoon, everyone. Today, we are going to discuss a fascinating concept in the realm of physics - time dilation. Time dilation refers to the phenomenon where time appears to move at different rates depending on relative motion or the strength of gravitational fields.

To understand time dilation, let's consider the theory of relativity proposed by Albert Einstein. According to this theory, time is not an absolute quantity but is instead relative to the observer's frame of reference. Time dilation occurs when different observers perceive time passing at different rates due to their relative motion or gravitational conditions.

One example where time dilation is evident is in the famous "twin paradox" scenario. Imagine two identical twins, one of whom embarks on a high-speed space journey while the other remains on Earth. Due to the relativistic effects of the journey, the twin traveling at high speeds experiences time moving slower compared to the twin on Earth. As a result, when the traveling twin returns, they will have aged less than their Earth-bound counterpart.

Time dilation is also observed in the presence of strong gravitational fields. For example, near a massive celestial body like a black hole, intense gravitational forces cause time to slow down. This effect is known as gravitational time dilation.

The concept of time dilation has been experimentally verified through various experiments and observations. For instance, high-precision atomic clocks on fast-moving airplanes or satellites have shown that time runs slightly slower for them compared to stationary clocks on Earth's surface.

Moreover, astronomical observations have revealed that objects near massive black holes experience significant time dilation. The gravitational pull of these massive objects warps the space-time fabric, resulting in time appearing to slow down as one approaches the event horizon.

Understanding time dilation is crucial for many areas of physics, including space travel, astrophysics, and the functioning of GPS systems. Failure to account for time dilation effects can lead to significant errors in calculations and measurements.

In conclusion, time dilation is a captivating phenomenon where time appears to move differently depending on relative motion or gravitational conditions. It is a fundamental concept in the theory of relativity and has profound implications for our understanding of the nature of time itself.

Thank you for your attention, and I hope this lecture has provided you with valuable insights into the fascinating world of time dilation.

[End of transcript]

Sample Excellent Response:

According to the lecture on the theory of relativity, time dilation is a phenomenon where time appears to move slower in a fast-moving object or in the presence of strong gravitational fields. As an object's velocity increases or as it approaches a massive celestial body, time is perceived differently relative to an observer in a different reference frame.

To understand the concept of time dilation, consider the scenario of two identical clocks - one stationary on Earth and one aboard a hypothetical spacecraft traveling at a significant fraction of the speed of light. According to the lecture, as the spacecraft accelerates and travels closer to the speed of light, time will pass slower for the astronauts aboard the spacecraft relative to those on Earth.

This time dilation effect is a consequence of the theory of relativity, which posits that the laws of physics are the same for all observers moving relative to each other. The lecture explains that as an object's speed approaches the speed of light, time for that object begins to slow down relative to a stationary observer.

The implications of time dilation for space travel are profound. As discussed in the lecture, astronauts traveling at high speeds or encountering strong gravitational fields experience time differently from observers on Earth. This means that time for the astronauts will appear to move slower compared to time experienced on Earth. This effect becomes more pronounced the closer the spacecraft's speed approaches the speed of light.

As a result, space travelers could potentially experience time dilation such that, upon returning to Earth after a long journey in space, they may have aged less compared to people on Earth. This phenomenon has been verified through experiments with atomic clocks on high-speed aircraft and satellites.

In conclusion, the lecture on the theory of relativity sheds light on the concept of time dilation and its implications for space travel. Time dilation manifests as a difference in the passage of time, where time appears to move slower in fast-moving objects or in the presence of strong gravitational fields. This effect has important implications for space travelers, as they may experience less time passing relative to observers on Earth. The concept of time dilation exemplifies the intricacies of the theory of relativity and its profound impact on our understanding of the universe.

Strategies for Test-Takers:

1. **Active listening and note-taking:** Focus on key points and explanations provided in the lecture. Take concise notes to ensure accuracy and facilitate a well-rounded response.

2. **Clearly define the concept:** Begin your response by providing a concise yet comprehensive explanation of time dilation. Ensure your response reflects an understanding of the phenomenon and its implications.

3. **Provide specific examples:** Use the example of clocks on a spacecraft traveling at high speeds versus stationary clocks on Earth to explain the concept of time dilation. This helps illustrate the effect and facilitate understanding.

4. **Connect to the theory of relativity:** Emphasize the relationship between time dilation and the theory of relativity, highlighting how time is relative to an observer's frame of reference. Incorporate relevant terminology and concepts from the lecture to showcase your comprehension.

5. **Use logical reasoning:** Build your response by logically explaining the cause-and-effect relationship between velocity, time dilation, and the experience of astronauts in space travel. Connect your arguments clearly and coherently.

6. **Manage time:** Effective time management is essential in delivering a comprehensive response within the given time limit. Allocate sufficient time for brainstorming, organizing your thoughts, and delivering a well-structured response.

7. **Practice pronunciation and fluency:** Pay attention to your pronunciation, intonation, and fluency when practicing. Aim for clear, articulate speech to ensure your response is easily understandable.

By engaging actively with the lecture, taking concise notes, and practicing these strategies, you will enhance your ability to understand complex physics concepts and deliver a well-crafted response in the TOEFL speaking section. Regular practice and continuous improvement will contribute to your success.

Sample Speaking Question -1

Task:

Imagine you are a student who has recently moved to a new city for studies. You are struggling to adjust to your new environment and make friends. Your university is organizing a cultural fair and they are looking for volunteers to help with different activities during the event. In your response, explain why you think volunteering at the fair would be a good opportunity for you.

Include details such as the benefits you expect to gain, the skills you possess that make you a suitable candidate, and how this experience could help you integrate better into your new community.

You will have 45 seconds to prepare and 60 seconds to respond.

Response:

Volunteering at the university's cultural fair would be a wonderful opportunity for me for several reasons. Firstly, it would provide me with a chance to meet new people and make friends. As a student who is struggling to adjust to the new environment, interacting with others during the fair would help me break the ice and establish connections with like-minded individuals who share similar interests in culture and diversity.

Moreover, volunteering at the cultural fair would allow me to gain valuable skills and experiences. I possess excellent communication skills that would enable me to engage with attendees and contribute to creating a positive and welcoming atmosphere at the event.

Additionally, my organizational skills and attention to detail would make me a suitable candidate for assisting in various activities, such as coordinating performances or managing exhibits.

Furthermore, this volunteering experience would assist me in integrating better into my new community. By actively participating in university events, I would have opportunities to learn more about the local culture, traditions, and values, which can help me better understand and appreciate my new surroundings.

Volunteering would also provide me with a sense of belonging and purpose, allowing me to actively contribute to the community and establish a positive reputation within it. Overall, volunteering at the cultural fair would not only benefit me personally by facilitating the process of adjusting to my new environment and making friends, but it would also allow me to develop important skills and contribute positively to my new community. I am excited about this opportunity and eager to take an active role in university events.

Sample Speaking Question - 2

Task:

You are a student who is taking a course on environmental sustainability. Your professor has assigned a group project where you and your team need to propose a solution to reduce plastic waste on your university campus. In your response, describe the current situation with plastic waste on campus, explain the proposal your team has developed, and discuss the potential benefits of implementing this solution. Provide specific details and reasons to support your argument.

You will have 45 seconds to prepare and 60 seconds to respond.

Response:

In our university campus, the issue of plastic waste is a pressing concern. The abundance of single-use plastic items, such as water bottles, food containers, and packaging, contributes to the growing environmental problem. Our team has developed a proposal to address this issue by implementing a comprehensive plastic recycling and reduction program.

Firstly, our proposal focuses on raising awareness and promoting behavior change. We plan to launch a campus-wide campaign to educate students, faculty, and detrimental effects of plastic waste and the importance of recycling. This campaign will include informative workshops, interactive displays, and informative signage placed strategically around campus to encourage sustainable practices.

Secondly, we aim to improve the waste management infrastructure on campus. This includes increasing the number of conveniently placed recycling bins for plastic items and implementing a separate collection system for plastic waste. Additionally, we plan to collaborate with local recycling facilities to ensure the captured plastic waste is properly processed and recycled.

By implementing our proposal, several benefits could be achieved. Firstly, there would be a significant reduction in plastic waste on campus, resulting in a cleaner and more sustainable environment. This reduction would also lead to a decrease in the consumption of single-use plastics, promoting a culture of reusable alternatives among the campus community.

Furthermore, the implementation of an efficient plastic recycling system would contribute to the circular economy by diverting plastic waste from landfills and reducing the reliance on virgin plastic production. This would help conserve resources and reduce carbon emissions associated with plastic production.

Additionally, our proposal offers an educational opportunity for students to actively engage and learn about sustainable practices. By involving students in the campaign and recycling initiatives, we would foster a sense of environmental stewardship and provide them with the knowledge and skills to implement sustainable practices throughout their lives.

In conclusion, our team's proposal to reduce plastic waste on campus emphasizes raising awareness, improving waste management infrastructure, and promoting behavior change. By implementing these measures, we aim to achieve a significant reduction in plastic waste, promote a reusable culture, and contribute to a cleaner and more environmentally sustainable campus. The benefits include a cleaner environment, resource conservation, reduced carbon emissions, and the cultivation of environmental literacy among the campus community.

Sample Speaking Question - 3

Transcript of Lecture (excerpt):

"In today's lecture, we explored the topic of renewable energy sources, focusing on solar power as a sustainable option. Solar energy offers numerous benefits, including being environmentally friendly, abundant, and renewable. However, there are also challenges associated with solar power, such as intermittency, high initial costs, and the need for storage solutions. As we assess the role of solar energy in our energy mix, it is essential to consider both its advantages and limitations.

Solar energy offers multiple benefits that make it an attractive choice. Firstly, solar power is environmentally friendly. Unlike fossil fuels, solar energy does not release harmful greenhouse gases into the atmosphere, contributing to climate change. It helps in reducing our carbon footprint and mitigating the impacts of global warming.

Secondly, solar energy is abundant and renewable. The sun is an abundant source of energy that is available in abundance every day. It provides a consistent and reliable source of power that can be harnessed for electricity generation. Unlike finite fossil fuel resources, solar energy is renewable and will not deplete as long as the sun continues to shine.

However, despite its advantages, solar power also faces challenges. One of the main challenges is intermittency. Solar power generation is dependent on sunlight, which is not available 24/7. It means that solar energy production fluctuates with the availability of sunlight, requiring storage solutions or complementary power sources to ensure a consistent energy supply.

Another challenge is the high initial costs associated with solar power installations. While the cost of solar technology has decreased over time, there are still significant upfront expenses involved in setting up solar panels, inverters, and other necessary infrastructure. However, it is important to note that these costs are often offset by long-term energy savings and the potential for government incentives.

To address these challenges, continued advancements in solar technology are necessary. Research and development efforts should focus on improving the efficiency of solar panels, developing more affordable storage solutions, and creating innovative ways to integrate solar power into the energy grid effectively.

In conclusion, solar power has numerous advantages as a sustainable source of energy. Its environmental benefits, abundance, and renewability make it an attractive option for a clean energy future. Nonetheless, challenges such as intermittency and high initial costs must be addressed through ongoing technological advancements. By embracing solar power and overcoming these challenges, we can accelerate the transition to a more sustainable and renewable energy landscape.

Question:

Based on the information provided in the lecture, discuss your opinion on whether solar power should be prioritized as the primary source of renewable energy in the future.

Support your response with evidence from the lecture and your own critical analysis.

You will have 45 seconds to prepare and 60 seconds to respond.

Response:

In my opinion, solar power should be prioritized as the primary source of renewable energy in the future. The lecture highlights several compelling reasons to support this viewpoint.

Firstly, solar power offers significant environmental benefits. It is a clean and sustainable energy source that does not release harmful greenhouse gases, unlike fossil fuels. By reducing our reliance on fossil fuels and transitioning to solar power, we can mitigate the negative impacts of climate change and contribute to a healthier and more sustainable planet.

Secondly, solar energy is abundant and renewable. The sun is an abundant source of energy, providing a consistent supply of power every day. Unlike finite fossil fuel resources, solar energy is indefinitely renewable as long as the sun continues to shine. This abundance makes solar power a reliable and long-term solution for our energy needs.

Furthermore, the lecture acknowledges the challenges associated with solar power, such as intermittency and high initial costs. However, these challenges can be addressed through technological advancements. Storage solutions, such as batteries, can help overcome the intermittency issue by storing excess solar power for use during periods of low sunlight.

Additionally, ongoing research and development efforts are improving the efficiency of solar panels and reducing the overall costs of installation.

From a critical analysis perspective, prioritizing solar power as the primary source of renewable energy aligns with the goals of transitioning to a low-carbon economy and achieving energy sustainability. Solar power has vast potential for scalability and can be integrated into various sectors, including residential, commercial, and industrial. Furthermore, implementing solar power on a large scale can create job opportunities, stimulate economic growth, and strengthen energy independence.

In conclusion, considering the environmental benefits, abundance, and renewability of solar power, it should be prioritized as the primary source of renewable energy in the future.

Addressing the challenges associated with solar power through technological advancements and policy support is crucial. By harnessing the power of the sun, we can foster a sustainable energy landscape and contribute to a cleaner and brighter future for generations to come.

Sample Speaking Question - 4

Transcript of Lecture (excerpt - continued):

"Furthermore, the loss of biodiversity not only threatens the delicate balance of ecosystems but also has profound implications for human well-being. Biodiversity loss can affect food security, ecosystem services, and even the discovery of new medicines derived from natural resources.

Preserving biodiversity is not merely an environmental concern but a critical aspect of sustaining life on Earth.

In light of these challenges, collaborative efforts are needed to address the dual crises of climate change and biodiversity loss. Individuals can contribute by adopting sustainable practices in their daily lives, supporting conservation efforts, and advocating for policies that prioritize environmental protection. At the governmental level, robust environmental policies, international cooperation, and investments in green technologies are essential to safeguarding biodiversity and combating climate change.

As we navigate these interconnected challenges, a holistic approach that integrates scientific research, community engagement, and policy interventions is key to fostering resilience andsustainability in the face of a changing climate. By valuing and preserving biodiversity, we can secure a healthier planet for present and future generations."

This extended excerpt elaborates on the impacts of climate change on global biodiversity and emphasizes the importance of collective action in addressing these environmental challenges effectively."

Question:

Based on the information provided in the lecture, discuss the interplay between human activities and climate change in relation to global biodiversity. How can individuals and governments collaborate to address these environmental issues effectively, and what role does public awareness and policy implementation play in preserving biodiversity amidst climate challenges? Provide examples and insights to support your response.

Response:

The lecture strongly highlights the interplay between human activities, climate change, and global biodiversity. Human actions, such as deforestation, habitat destruction, and the release of greenhouse gases, contribute to climate change, which in turn has detrimental effects on biodiversity.

The impacts of climate change on biodiversity are far-reaching. The lecture points out that loss of biodiversity disrupts ecosystems and can have significant implications for human well-being. For instance, it affects food security as agricultural systems rely on diverse species for pollination, pest control, and nutrient cycling. Biodiversity loss also threatens ecosystem services, such as clean water, air purification, flood control, and climate regulation. Additionally, the decline in biodiversity hinders the discovery of potentially life-saving medicines derived from natural resources.

To address these interconnected challenges, collaboration between individuals and governments is crucial. Individuals can make a difference by adopting sustainable practices in their daily lives, such as reducing waste, conserving energy, supporting local and sustainable food systems, and engaging in responsible consumer choices. Additionally, individuals can contribute by supporting conservation efforts, volunteering with environmental organizations, and advocating for policies that prioritize environmental protection.

At the governmental level, strong environmental policies are necessary to address climate change and biodiversity loss. Governments can implement regulations to curb greenhouse gas emissions, protect critical habitats, and promote sustainable land use practices. International cooperation is essential, as these environmental issues transcend national boundaries. Collaborative efforts, such as the Paris Agreement, facilitate global action and target reductions in greenhouse gas emissions.

Public awareness plays a crucial role in preserving biodiversity amidst climate challenges. Education and outreach programs can raise awareness about the value and importance of biodiversity, highlighting its connection to human well-being. By understanding the significance of biodiversity, individuals can become advocates for conservation and encourage others to take action.

In conclusion, the interplay between human activities, climate change, and global biodiversity is evident. Addressing these environmental challenges requires collaboration between individuals and governments. Individuals can contribute through sustainable practices and advocacy, while governments need to implement robust policies and engage in international cooperation. By raising public awareness, preserving biodiversity can become a collective responsibility, securing a healthier planet for future generations.

Sample Speaking Question - 5

Conversation:

Person A: Hey, have you heard about the new recycling program our city is implementing?

Person B: Yes, I have! I think it's a great initiative to reduce waste and promote sustainability.

Person A: Absolutely! They mentioned something about separating recyclables into different categories. Do you know which items are included in each category?

Person B: Yes, there are typically three categories: paper and cardboard, plastic and glass containers, and metal cans. It's important to sort our recyclables correctly to ensure effective recycling.

Person A: That's good to know. I want to make sure I'm doing it right. By the way, do you know if they will provide separate bins for each category?

Person B: Yes, they will. The city will distribute color-coded bins for each category, making the sorting process easier for residents.

Question: Based on the conversation, summarize the main points about the new recycling program and its implementation. Then, discuss the importance of correctly sorting recyclables into different categories and explain how the provision of color-coded bins can facilitate this process. Support your response with details from the dialogue and your own insights.

You will have 45 seconds to prepare and 60 seconds to respond.

Response:

The conversation focuses on the new recycling program being implemented in the city. The program aims to reduce waste and promote sustainability. Recyclables need to be sorted into three main categories: paper and cardboard, plastic and glass containers, and metal cans.

Correctly sorting recyclables is crucial for effective recycling. The city will provide color-coded bins for each category, making the sorting process easier for residents.

Proper sorting of recyclables into different categories is essential for efficient recycling.

By separating recyclables based on their material type, it allows for more streamlined and effective recycling processes. It ensures that each type of material can undergo the appropriate recycling method, maximizing the recovery of resources and minimizing waste.

The provision of color-coded bins for each category simplifies the sorting process for residents. The visual distinction helps individuals quickly identify which bin to use for specific recyclables. This reduces confusion and the likelihood of incorrect sorting, improving the overall efficiency of the recycling program.

Furthermore, the color-coded bins promote community engagement and participation in recycling efforts. Residents are more likely to embrace recycling when the process is made convenient and accessible. The clear guidance provided by the color-coded bins encourages consistency in recycling practices throughout the community.

In conclusion, the implementation of the new recycling program brings a positive change by promoting sustainability. Correctly sorting recyclables into different categories is crucial for effective recycling. The provision of color-coded bins simplifies the sorting process, making recycling more accessible and encouraging community participation. Through these efforts, the city aims to reduce waste, preserve resources, and create a more sustainable future.

Sample Speaking Question - 6

Conversation:

Person A: Did you hear about the controversial decision to build a new shopping mall in our neighborhood?

Person B: Yes, I did. Many people in the community are divided on this issue.

Person A: I understand there are concerns about the impact on the environment and local businesses. Could you elaborate on some of those concerns?

Person B: One concern is the potential destruction of green spaces and habitats for wildlife. Another is the potential loss of business for small, locally owned shops in the area.

Person A: That's true. On the other hand, proponents argue that the mall will bring additional job opportunities and boost the economy. What are some of the reasons they give to support their stance?

Person B: Supporters believe that the new mall will attract more visitors to the area, resulting in increased revenue for businesses and overall economic growth. They also argue that it will provide employment opportunities for local residents.

Question:

Based on the conversation, summarize the conflicting viewpoints regarding the construction of the shopping mall in the neighborhood. Identify and discuss the environmental and socio-economic concerns associated with the project. State your own stance on the issue, providing reasons and evidence to support your viewpoint.

You will have 45 seconds to prepare and 60 seconds to respond.

Response:

The conversation revolves around the conflicting viewpoints regarding the construction of a shopping mall in the neighborhood. Some concerns raised include potential environmental impacts, such as the destruction of green spaces and wildlife habitats, as well as the adverse effects on small, locally-owned businesses. On the other hand, proponents argue that the mall will bring job opportunities and economic growth to the area.

From an environmental perspective, the construction of a shopping mall could lead to the loss of important green spaces, potentially harming local ecosystems and wildlife habitats. This destruction could have long-term consequences for biodiversity and the overall health of the environment.

Socio-economically, the establishment of a new mall raises concerns about the negative impact on small, locally-owned businesses in the area. The competition posed by larger, more well- funded chain stores within the mall could lead to the decline or closure of these smaller businesses, resulting in a loss of diversity and character within the local community.

On the other hand, supporters argue that the mall would bring economic benefits to the area. They believe that the increased foot traffic and visitors attracted to the mall would stimulate local businesses, leading to increased revenue and employment opportunities for local residents. This economic growth has the potential to boost the overall prosperity and development of the neighborhood.

In my opinion, while economic growth and job opportunities are important, it is crucial to consider the long-term environmental and socio-economic impacts. Sustainable development should be prioritized, finding a balance between economic growth and environmental preservation. It is essential to explore alternative solutions, such as repurposing existing structures or revitalizing vacant spaces, which can promote economic growth while minimizing the negative impacts on the environment and local businesses.

In conclusion, the construction of a shopping mall in the neighborhood stirs conflicting viewpoints. Environmental concerns include the potential destruction of green spaces and habitats, while socio-economic concerns relate to the impact on small, local businesses.

Balancing economic growth with environmental sustainability is essential. By exploring alternative solutions and adopting sustainable practices, we can prioritize both the well-being of the environment and the long-term economic prosperity of the community.

Sample Speaking Question - 7

Transcript of Lecture (excerpt):

"In today's lecture, we explored the concept of genetically modified organisms (GMOs) and their role in agriculture. GMOs are created by altering the genetic makeup of organisms, such as plants, to enhance desirable traits. While GMOs have been instrumental in increasing crop yields and addressing food security challenges, they have also raised concerns about potential environmental impacts and long-term health effects. Understanding the benefits and risks of GMOs is crucial for making informed decisions about their use.

Environmental impacts are a major consideration, as GMOs may interfere with natural ecosystems and harm biodiversity. Additionally, there are potential health risks associated with the consumption of genetically modified crops, although extensive studies have not yet provided conclusive evidence of negative effects. It is crucial to conduct comprehensive research to understand any potential long-term health impacts.

To ensure the responsible use of GMOs, it is suggested that implementing stringent regulations and monitoring systems is beneficial. Increased transparency in labeling GMO products can provide consumers with informed choices. Rigorous risk assessments, ongoing research, and public dialogue are vital to address concerns and mitigate any potential negative effects.

In summary, responsible implementation, research, and informed decision-making play crucial roles in maximizing the benefits of GMOs while minimizing risks and ensuring sustainability in agriculture."

Question:

Based on the information provided in the lecture, discuss the advantages and potential drawbacks of genetically modified organisms in agriculture. Evaluate the environmental and health considerations associated with GMOs, and propose strategies or approaches to ensure their responsible use. Support your response with evidence from the lecture and your own critical analysis.

You will have 45 seconds to prepare and 60 seconds to respond.

Response:

Genetically modified organisms (GMOs) in agriculture have both advantages and potential drawbacks, as outlined in the lecture. One major benefit is their ability to increase crop yields, addressing food security challenges and alleviating hunger in many parts of the world. By enhancing desirable traits, GMOs can create crops that are more resistant to pests, diseases, and environmental stressors, ensuring consistent and healthy food production.

However, there are environmental considerations associated with GMOs. They may disrupt natural ecosystems, leading to potential harm to biodiversity and ecological balance. The introduction of GMO crops can have unintended consequences, such as the unintended spread of modified genes to wild plants or the development of resistant pests. Careful monitoring, regulation, and risk assessments can help mitigate these risks and ensure environmental sustainability.

Another aspect of concern is the potential health impacts of consuming genetically modified crops. While extensive studies have not provided conclusive evidence of negative effects, it is crucial to prioritize comprehensive research and ongoing monitoring. Robust risk assessments should be conducted to ensure the safety of GMO crops and to address any potential long-term health impacts.

To ensure the responsible use of GMOs, several strategies can be implemented. Stringent regulations, monitoring systems, and increased transparency through proper labeling of GMO products can empower consumers to make informed choices. Rigorous risk assessments and ongoing research are essential to address any concerns and provide scientific evidence on the safety and impact of GMOs.

Furthermore, it is important to foster public dialogue and engagement to ensure that the opinions and concerns of various stakeholders, including farmers, scientists, and consumers, are taken into account. By promoting transparency, knowledge sharing, and inclusive decision-making processes, responsible use and management of GMOs in agriculture can be achieved.

In conclusion, GMOs in agriculture offer benefits such as increased crop yields and food security. However, environmental and health considerations must be addressed to ensure responsible use. Strategies such as regulation, monitoring, transparency, ongoing research, and inclusive decision-making can help mitigate risks and maximize the benefits of GMOs while ensuring sustainability in agriculture.

Sample Speaking Question - 8

Question:
In today's interconnected world, social media has become an integral part of our lives, offering both advantages and disadvantages. Based on your own observations and experiences, what is your opinion on the overall impact of social media on society?

In your response, clearly state your viewpoint and provide reasons and examples to support your stance. Consider the effects of social media on communication, relationships, information dissemination, privacy, and mental well-being. Additionally, discuss any potential strategies or approaches individuals and society can adopt to maximize the benefits and minimize the drawbacks of social media use.

You will have 45 seconds to prepare and 60 seconds to respond.

Response:
In my opinion, the overall impact of social media on society is both positive and negative. While social media has undoubtedly revolutionized communication and information dissemination, it also presents challenges and potential drawbacks.

On one hand, social media has enhanced communication by connecting people across the globe, breaking down geographical barriers, and fostering the exchange of ideas. It enables individuals to stay connected with friends and family, especially in today's fast-paced world. Additionally, social media platforms have become vital tools for sharing information, raising awareness about important social issues, and promoting social movements.

However, there are also negative aspects to consider. The constant exposure to curated content on social media can lead to a distorted view of reality and unrealistic expectations. It has the potential to foster feelings of inadequacy and contribute to a decline in mental well-being.

Furthermore, the spread of misinformation and fake news through social media platforms can have a detrimental impact on society and undermine the veracity of information.

To maximize the benefits of social media while minimizing the drawbacks, individuals can adopt certain strategies. This includes exercising critical thinking when consuming content, verifying information before sharing, and being mindful of the impact of social media on mental well- being. Society can play a role by promoting digital literacy and responsible social media use through education and awareness campaigns.

In conclusion, social media has brought undeniable advantages in terms of communication and information dissemination. However, there are also challenges to navigate, such as the distortion of reality and the spread of misinformation. By promoting responsible use, critical thinking, and digital literacy, individuals and society can harness the benefits of social media while mitigating the potential negative impacts.

Sample Speaking Question - 9

Conversation:

Person A: Have you heard about the recent surge in online shopping?

Person B: Yes, it seems like more people are opting for the convenience of online shopping these days.

Person A: Definitely. However, I've also heard concerns about the impact on local brick-and- mortar stores. What are some potential challenges they face due to the rise in online shopping?

Person B: One big challenge is competition. Online retailers often offer lower prices and a wider range of options, making it difficult for physical stores to attract customers. Additionally, maintaining an online presence or transitioning to e-commerce can be costly for small businesses.

Person A: That makes sense. On the other hand, online shopping offers benefits like accessibility and convenience. Are there any ways for local stores to adapt and thrive in this digital age?

Person B: Absolutely! Some local stores have turned to offering unique in-store experiences, personalized customer service, or niche products to differentiate themselves from online giants. Additionally, creating an online presence, utilizing social media platforms, and implementing click-and-collect services can help bridge the gap between physical and digital retail.

Question:

Based on the conversation, summarize the challenges faced by local brick-and-mortar stores due to the rise in online shopping. Discuss potential strategies or approaches that physical stores can employ to remain competitive and thrive in the digital age. Support your response with details from the dialogue and your own insights.

You will have 45 seconds to prepare and 60 seconds to respond.

Response:

Local brick-and-mortar stores face significant challenges in the face of the rising popularity of online shopping. One of the major hurdles is the competition posed by online retailers, who often offer lower prices and a wider selection of products. This makes it difficult for physical stores to attract and retain customers. Additionally, the costs associated with establishing and maintaining an online presence can be a significant barrier, particularly for small businesses with limited resources.

However, despite these challenges, there are strategies that physical stores can employ to remain competitive and thrive in the digital age. One approach is to focus on providing unique in-store experiences that cannot be replicated by online retailers. This could involve creating an inviting and immersive atmosphere, offering personalized customer service, or hosting events and workshops that engage customers on a deeper level.

Furthermore, local stores can leverage their expertise and connections to offer niche products that cater to specific customer needs or interests. By specializing in a particular area, they can differentiate themselves from online giants and attract a loyal customer base seeking specialized products or services.

To bridge the gap between the physical and digital retail worlds, local stores should also establish an online presence. This could include setting up a website, utilizing social media platforms to engage with customers, and implementing click-and-collect services that allow customers to order online and pick up items at the store. This not only offers the convenience of online shopping but also drives foot traffic to the physical store.

In conclusion, while the rise of online shopping poses challenges for local brick-and-mortar stores, they can adapt and thrive by focusing on unique in-store experiences, offering niche products, establishing an online presence, and utilizing click-and-collect services. By leveraging their physical advantages and combining them with the convenience and personal touch of online shopping, local stores can remain competitive and continue to provide value to customers in the digital age.

Sample Speaking Question - 10

Question:

In recent years, there has been a growing discussion about the benefits and drawbacks of remote work. Based on your own experiences and observations, what is your opinion on the overall impact of remote work on individuals and organizations?

In your response, clearly state your viewpoint and provide reasons and examples to support your stance. Consider the effects of remote work on productivity, work-life balance, collaboration, and employee satisfaction. Additionally, discuss any potential challenges or considerations that should be addressed to optimize remote work arrangements for both individuals and organizations.

You will have 45 seconds to prepare and 60 seconds to respond.

Response:

In my opinion, remote work has had a largely positive impact on individuals and organizations. Firstly, remote work allows for increased flexibility and work-life balance. Employees can design their work schedule around personal obligations and have more control over their daily routine. This flexibility improves job satisfaction and reduces stress levels, ultimately leading to increased productivity.

Secondly, remote work has shown to boost employee productivity. With the absence of office distractions and the ability to create a personalized work environment, individuals can focus on their tasks and deliver high-quality work. Additionally, remote work eliminates commuting time, allowing employees to allocate that time for work-related activities, thus enhancing productivity.

Moreover, remote work has fueled a higher level of collaboration through advanced technology. Virtual meetings, project management platforms, and instant messaging tools allow teams to connect seamlessly from different locations. The ease of communication fosters a sense of teamwork, enabling employees to collaborate effectively despite physical distance.

However, there are challenges associated with remote work that should be addressed. Maintaining work-life boundaries can be difficult for some individuals, leading to longer work hours and potential burnout. Organizations should encourage setting boundaries and promoting a healthy work-life balance. Additionally, ensuring reliable and efficient technology infrastructure is crucial for seamless remote collaboration.

In conclusion, remote work has proven to be beneficial for individuals and organizations. It enhances work-life balance, boosts productivity, enables effective collaboration, and improves employee satisfaction. By addressing challenges such as work-life boundaries and technological considerations, remote work arrangements can be optimized to maximize its benefits for both individuals and organizations.

Writing Section

How to master the writing section?

The TOEFL writing section is a critical component of the examination that assesses a test-taker's ability to communicate effectively in written English. This section evaluates not only grammatical accuracy and vocabulary usage but also the candidate's capacity to produce well- organized and coherent responses within a given time limit of 30 minutes for each question.

The format of the TOEFL writing section consists of two tasks: an integrated writing task and an independent writing task. In the integrated writing task, candidates read a passage and listen to a related lecture. They are then asked to summarize the main points from both sources and demonstrate the relationship between them in a well-structured essay. The independent writing task requires test-takers to express their own opinion on a given topic and provide supporting evidence and examples to validate their viewpoint in a cogent and structured manner.

Scoring for the TOEFL writing section is based on a holistic rubric that takes into account various factors. These include the development of ideas, organization, clarity of expression, language use, and overall coherence. Both the integrated and independent tasks are scored on a scale of 0 to 5, and the final scores are converted into a total writing score of 0 to 30.

To excel in the TOEFL writing section, thorough preparation is essential. It is important to familiarize oneself with the task formats and practice integrating information from multiple sources in the integrated task. Developing strong critical thinking skills, as well as building a solid foundation in grammar and vocabulary, can aid in crafting well-reasoned arguments and effectively communicating ideas.

Additionally, time management plays a vital role during the actual test. Allocating sufficient time for planning, writing, and editing is crucial to produce a well-structured and error-free essay.

Practicing timed writing exercises and seeking feedback from teachers or peers can help improve overall performance. The strategies for mastering the writing section are:

- **Understand the Task:**
  - ➢ Carefully read and comprehend the instructions of each task to ensure a clear understanding of the requirements.
  - ➢ Read the prompt multiple times to grasp the main ideas and identify any specific instructions or questions.
  - ➢ Analyze the task type (integrated or independent) and understand the expectations for each task.

- **Plan Your Response:**
  - ➢ Brainstorm ideas and create an outline before starting the essay.
  - ➢ Organize main points and supporting details effectively to ensure coherence and logical progression.
  - ➢ Allocate time to plan, outline, and structure your essay, leaving sufficient time for writing and editing.

- **Develop Strong Theses and Arguments:**
  - ➢ Clearly state your thesis or main idea to provide a foundation for your essay.
  - ➢ Support your arguments with relevant examples, evidence, and reasoning.
  - ➢ Demonstrate critical thinking by presenting a balanced perspective and considering counterarguments.

- **Coherent and Cohesive Writing:**
  - ➢ Use appropriate transitional phrases and linking words to ensure smooth transitions between sentences and paragraphs.
  - ➢ Establish clear connections between ideas and paragraphs to maintain coherence and to enhance the flow of your essay.
  - ➢ Include topic sentences to introduce each paragraph and provide a clear focus.

- **Language Use and Grammar:**
  - ➢ Demonstrate a wide range of vocabulary and use precise terminology when appropriate.
  - ➢ Maintain grammatical accuracy and sentence structure variety.
  - ➢ Show a good command of sentence complexity, including the use of complex, compound, and simple sentences.

- **Time Management:**
  - Allocate sufficient time for planning, writing, and proofreading in order to deliver a well-structured and error-free essay.
  - Practice writing under timed conditions to improve speed and efficiency.

- **Edit and Revise:**
  - Set aside time at the end to review and edit your essay. o Check for grammar, spelling, and punctuation errors. o Ensure clarity, coherence, and relevance of ideas.

Sample Writing Question - 1

Writing Task:

In recent years, many governments and organizations have implemented measures to promote sustainability and combat climate change. Some argue that individuals should take personal responsibility for environmental protection, while others believe that governmental regulations are essential for creating significant change.

In an essay, discuss your opinion on the role of individuals versus government in addressing environmental issues. Support your viewpoint with relevant examples and evidence, and consider potential benefits and drawbacks of each approach. Additionally, explain how collaboration between individuals and government can lead to more effective and sustainable solutions to global environmental challenges.

You will have 30 minutes to plan, write, and revise your response. Your essay should be approximately 300-350 words in length.

Excellent Response:

In addressing the question about the role of individuals versus government in addressing environmental issues, it is important to recognize the significance of both. While individuals have the power to make personal choices that contribute to sustainability, government regulations play a crucial role in driving systematic change on a larger scale.

On one hand, individual actions can have a collective impact on the environment. Small, everyday choices such as reducing personal carbon footprint, conserving resources, and adopting sustainable practices can contribute to a healthier planet. For instance, opting for public transportation, recycling, or supporting local and sustainable products can make a difference.

Individuals have the ability to set examples, influence others, and create a culture of environmental responsibility.

However, the magnitude of environmental challenges requires comprehensive and systematic approaches that only governments can provide. Government regulations and policies can enforce environmental standards, invest in renewable energy, and promote sustainable practices across sectors. They can set emissions targets, develop conservation efforts, and enact legislation that safeguards natural resources. Furthermore, governments possess the authority and resources to allocate funding for research and development of eco-friendly technologies.

Although individual actions are significant, they alone cannot address complex global challenges like climate change. Effecting change at scale requires collaboration between individuals and government. By combining individual responsibility and government actions, a virtuous cycle can be established. Governments can support and incentivize sustainable practices through tax breaks and subsidies, while individuals can actively engage in civil society and advocate for stronger environmental policies.

In conclusion, both individuals and governments have important roles to play in addressing environmental issues. While individuals can contribute through personal choices and setting examples, governments have the power to enact regulations, drive systemic change, and mobilize resources at a larger scale. By combining individual responsibility with government actions, we can create a sustainable future for ourselves and generations to come.

Sample Writing Question - 2

Writing Task:

In today's digital age, social media has become a prominent platform for communication and self-expression. However, its pervasive presence raises questions about its impact on personal relationships and well-being.

In an essay, discuss the advantages and disadvantages of social media in terms of interpersonal connections and individual mental health. Provide examples and evidence to support your arguments, and consider factors such as social isolation, comparison, privacy concerns, and the ability to connect with others. Additionally, suggest strategies or approaches individuals can adopt to maintain a healthy balance in their social media usage while nurturing meaningful relationships.

You will have 30 minutes to plan, write, and revise your response. Your essay should be approximately 300-350 words in length.

Excellent Response:

Social media undoubtedly has both advantages and disadvantages when it comes to interpersonal connections and individual mental health.

On one hand, social media offers numerous benefits for interpersonal connections. It provides a platform for people to connect and communicate with friends, family, and even strangers across the globe. Through social media, individuals can maintain long-distance relationships, share experiences and updates, and discover common interests. It allows people to connect with others who share similar hobbies or passions, creating communities and fostering a sense of belonging.

However, social media also presents certain challenges to interpersonal connections and mental health. One major concern is the potential for social isolation. Excessive use of social media can lead individuals to substitute online interactions for real-life socializing, impacting their ability to form and maintain deep emotional connections. Moreover, the curated and idealized nature of social media feeds can lead to feelings of inadequacy and comparison with others, contributing to diminished self-esteem and mental health issues.

Privacy concerns are another drawback of social media platforms. With the vast amount of personal information shared online, individuals may become vulnerable to privacy breaches and misuse of their data. This can lead to anxiety and distrust, affecting their overall well-being.

To maintain a healthy balance in social media usage and nurture meaningful relationships, individuals can adopt several strategies. First, it is important to be mindful of the time spent on social media platforms and set limits to avoid excessive usage. Engaging in offline activities, such as hobbies, sports, and face-to-face interactions, can help individuals cultivate real-life connections. Additionally, being selective about the content consumed and actively curating one's social media feed can promote a positive and supportive online environment.

In conclusion, while social media offers opportunities for interpersonal connections, it also poses challenges to personal relationships and mental well-being. Striking a balance between online and offline interactions, being mindful of usage, and cultivating authentic connections can mitigate the negative effects of social media and promote healthier relationships and well-being.

Sample Writing Question - 3

Writing Task:

In contemporary society, the influence of mass media is undeniable, shaping our perceptions, opinions, and behaviors. However, this influence has sparked debates about the accuracy and reliability of information provided by the media.

Write an essay discussing the advantages and disadvantages of mass media in shaping public opinion. Provide examples and evidence to support your arguments, considering factors such as the role of media in democratic societies, the potential for bias and misinformation, and the impact of media on social and political issues. Additionally, propose strategies or approaches individuals can adopt to navigate the complex media landscape and critically evaluate the information they encounter.

You will have 30 minutes to plan, write, and revise your response. Aim for an essay length of approximately 300-350 words.

Excellent Response:

Mass media plays a significant role in shaping public opinion, but its influence comes with both advantages and disadvantages.

On one hand, mass media serves as a crucial source of information and an important platform for public discourse in democratic societies. It facilitates the dissemination of news, providing access to a wide range of topics and perspectives. By presenting different viewpoints and holding those in power accountable, media can contribute to an informed citizenry and foster a healthy democracy. Furthermore, media coverage of social and political issues can create awareness and mobilize public support for positive change.

However, there are several drawbacks to consider when examining the impact of mass media on public opinion. A key concern is the potential for bias and misinformation. Media outlets may have their own agendas, leading to a distortion of facts or a one-sided portrayal of events. This can manipulate public perceptions and undermine the democratic process. Additionally, sensationalism and the prioritization of clickbait can result in shallow coverage, oversimplification, and a lack of nuanced analysis.

To navigate the complex media landscape and critically evaluate the information encountered, individuals can adopt several strategies. First and foremost, it is essential to consume news from diverse and reputable sources, verifying facts and cross-referencing information. Developing media literacy skills, including the ability to discern bias and identify reliable sources, is crucial. Actively engaging in media literacy education programs and fostering critical thinking can empower individuals to make informed judgments and avoid falling victim to misinformation.

In conclusion, mass media holds considerable power in shaping public opinion. While it offers access to information, diverse perspectives, and the potential for positive societal change, there are inherent challenges like bias and misinformation. By actively engaging with media and developing critical thinking skills, individuals can navigate the media landscape, separate fact from fiction, and contribute to a better-informed society.

Sample Writing Question - 4

Writing Task:

In today's globalized world, there is an ongoing debate about the impact of cultural diversity on society. In an essay, discuss the advantages and disadvantages of embracing cultural diversity in communities. Provide examples and evidence to support your arguments, considering factors such as social cohesion, creativity, economic benefits, and potential challenges related to cultural clashes or social divisions. Additionally, propose strategies or approaches that individuals and communities can adopt to promote inclusivity and harness the benefits of cultural diversity.

You will have 30 minutes to plan, write, and revise your response. Aim for an essay length of approximately 300-350 words.

Excellent Response:

Cultural diversity in communities has both advantages and disadvantages, and understanding and embracing its impact is crucial for an inclusive and harmonious society.

Embracing cultural diversity brings numerous benefits to communities. Firstly, it fosters social cohesion by promoting understanding, empathy, and tolerance among individuals from different backgrounds. Exposure to diverse cultures encourages individuals to challenge stereotypes and prejudices, leading to a more inclusive and harmonious community. Additionally, cultural diversity enhances creativity and innovation. When individuals from various cultural backgrounds come together, their unique perspectives, knowledge, and experiences can spark new ideas and solutions, leading to economic growth and development.

However, cultural diversity can also present challenges. Cultural clashes or misunderstandings may arise, leading to social divisions and conflicts within communities. Differences in language, customs, and values can create barriers to effective communication and collaboration. In some cases, cultural diversity may be perceived as a threat to social cohesion, and efforts to maintain cultural identities may hinder integration and hinder the development of a cohesive community.

To harness the benefits of cultural diversity while addressing its challenges, communities can adopt several strategies. First and foremost, fostering intercultural dialogue and education is essential. Promoting cultural awareness and understanding can help break down barriers and build bridges between different cultural groups. Moreover, creating platforms and events that celebrate and showcase diverse cultures can encourage appreciation and stronger connections among community members.

In conclusion, embracing cultural diversity brings numerous advantages to communities, including social cohesion and innovation. However, challenges such as cultural clashes and social divisions also need to be addressed. By promoting intercultural dialogue, education, and celebratory events, communities can create an inclusive environment that harnesses the benefits of cultural diversity while promoting unity and harmony.

Sample Writing Question - 5

Writing Task:

In recent years, there has been a growing concern about the impact of fast fashion on the environment, labor conditions, and sustainability. In an essay, discuss the advantages and disadvantages of the fast fashion industry. Provide examples and evidence to support your arguments, considering factors such as environmental impact, exploitation of labor, disposable consumer culture, and the potential for promoting ethical and sustainable fashion practices.

Additionally, propose strategies or approaches that individuals and the fashion industry can adopt to mitigate the negative effects and promote sustainable fashion choices.

You will have 30 minutes to plan, write, and revise your response. Aim for an essay length of approximately 300-350 words.

Excellent Response:

The fast fashion industry has both advantages and disadvantages, and understanding its impact is essential in promoting sustainable and ethical practices.

On the positive side, fast fashion brings affordability and accessibility to consumers. It allows individuals to stay up-to-date with the latest fashion trends at an affordable price point. Fast fashion retailers provide a wide variety of clothing options and cater to diverse consumer preferences. Additionally, the industry stimulates economic growth and job opportunities, especially in developing countries where garment production is a significant source of employment.

However, there are concerns surrounding the fast fashion industry. One major drawback is its detrimental environmental impact. Fast fashion relies on rapid production and consumption, leading to excessive resource use, pollution, and waste generation. The production of synthetic fibers and chemical dyes contributes to water pollution and carbon emissions, while the disposal of garments contributes to landfill problems.

Moreover, the fast fashion industry is often criticized for labor exploitation. Low wages, poor working conditions, and limited labor rights are prevalent in many fast fashion supply chains. Workers, especially those overseas, often face long working hours and are subjected to unsafe environments, which raises ethical concerns and violates human rights.

To mitigate the negative effects of the fast fashion industry, individuals and the fashion industry must take steps towards sustainability and ethical practices. Consumers can promote slow fashion by buying durable, high-quality clothing and embracing a more conscious and minimalistic approach to consumption. Supporting brands that prioritize ethical sourcing, fair wages, and environmentally friendly production processes can drive positive change.

Similarly, the fashion industry needs to prioritize sustainability by adopting more responsible practices. This includes using eco-friendly materials, implementing waste reduction strategies, promoting transparency throughout the supply chain, and supporting fair labor practices.

Furthermore, promoting upcycling, recycling, and garment rental services can contribute to reducing fashion waste.

In conclusion, the fast fashion industry brings both advantages and disadvantages. While it provides affordability and accessibility, it also poses significant environmental and ethical challenges. By adopting sustainable and ethical practices as individuals and within the fashion industry, we can promote a more responsible and conscious approach to fashion consumption, fostering a more sustainable and ethical future for the industry.

Sample Integrated Writing Task - 1

Integrated Writing Task:

Read the excerpt below from a lecture on the benefits of exercise, then listen to a related podcast segment. Summarize the main points made in the lecture and the podcast segment. Explain how the speaker in the podcast supports or challenges the ideas presented in the lecture.

Lecture Excerpt (reading passage):

Regular exercise has numerous benefits for physical and mental health. It reduces the risk of chronic diseases, improves cardiovascular health, and enhances cognitive function. Exercise also plays a vital role in maintaining healthy body weight and promoting overall well-being.

Regular exercise is not just a helpful habit but also a fundamental factor in maintaining good physical and mental health. Engaging in physical activity brings about numerous benefits that contribute to an overall sense of well-being.

One of the primary advantages of regular exercise is a reduced risk of chronic diseases. Research has shown that individuals who maintain an active lifestyle are less prone to conditions such as heart disease, diabetes, and obesity. Physical activity helps to regulate blood pressure, improve cholesterol levels, and enhance insulin sensitivity, all of which have a positive impact on long-term health outcomes.

Additionally, exercise improves cardiovascular health. Aerobic activities like jogging, swimming, or cycling strengthen the heart and improve its efficiency in pumping blood throughout the body. This leads to increased stamina, better endurance, and a reduced risk of cardiovascular diseases.

Exercise has also been linked to enhanced cognitive function. Engaging in physical activity increases blood flow to the brain, improving oxygen and nutrient delivery, leading to better cognitive performance and memory. Regular exercise has also been associated with a reduced risk of age-related cognitive decline and neurodegenerative diseases.

Beyond the physical benefits, exercise plays a crucial role in maintaining a healthy body weight. It helps to burn calories, build lean muscle mass, and boost metabolism. By incorporating physical activity into a balanced lifestyle, individuals can manage their weight more effectively and reduce the risk of obesity-related conditions.

Furthermore, exercise contributes to overall well-being by promoting mental health. Physical activity releases endorphins, known as "feel-good" hormones, which can uplift mood and reduce symptoms of stress, anxiety, and depression. It also provides an outlet for stress relief, promotes better sleep, and boosts self-esteem and body image.

In conclusion, regular exercise offers a myriad of benefits for physical and mental health. It reduces the risk of chronic diseases, improves cardiovascular health, enhances cognitive function, helps maintain a healthy body weight, and promotes overall well-being. By incorporating exercise into one's routine, individuals can enjoy a higher quality of life and reduce the likelihood of developing various health conditions.

Podcast Segment (listening passage - transcript):

Host: Welcome back to our podcast series on health and well-being. In today's episode, we have a special guest, Dr. Jane Simmons, who will be sharing insights on the importance of holistic well-being beyond exercise. Welcome, Dr. Simmons.

Dr. Simmons: Thank you for having me. It's a pleasure to be here.

Host: Dr. Simmons, many people consider exercise as the key to good health. Could you shed light on whether exercise alone guarantees overall well-being?

Dr. Simmons: Absolutely. Exercise is undoubtedly beneficial for our health, but it is only

one piece of the puzzle when it comes to overall well-being. We need to take a holistic approach and consider various factors that contribute to good health.

Host: Could you elaborate on these additional factors that are critical for overall well-being?

Dr. Simmons: Certainly. First, genetics plays a significant role in determining our health outcomes. We all have different predispositions to certain conditions, and our genetic makeup can influence how exercise affects our bodies. Additionally, diet is crucial. No matter how much we exercise, an unhealthy diet can have adverse effects on our well-being. A balanced and nutritious diet is essential for optimal health.

Furthermore, mental well-being should not be overlooked. Our emotional and psychological state can significantly impact our overall health. Stress management, mindfulness, and fostering positive relationships are essential for a healthy mind, which in turn affects the body. Neglecting mental well-being can undermine the benefits of exercise alone.

Host: It's evident that exercise is just one piece of a larger puzzle for overall well-being. How can individuals approach these additional factors alongside exercise?

Dr. Simmons: To achieve optimum health, individuals should adopt a holistic mindset. Incorporate regular exercise into your routine while also considering genetic factors and making conscious dietary choices. It's important to prioritize mental well-being by engaging in stress- reduction activities, practicing self-care, and seeking support when needed. By addressing all these aspects, individuals can attain a more comprehensive and sustainable state of well-being.

Host: Thank you, Dr. Simmons, for sharing your valuable insights on overall well-being beyond exercise. It's clear that exercise alone is not the sole determinant of good health, and considering genetic, dietary, and mental well-being factors is essential for a holistic approach to well-being.

Dr. Simmons: Thank you for having me. I hope this discussion encourages individuals to adopt a well-rounded approach to health and prioritize all aspects of their well-being.

Host: And that brings us to the end of this episode. Thank you all for tuning in, and we hope you found this conversation enlightening. Stay tuned for our next episode on further exploring the journey to wellness.

Answer:

According to the lecture, exercise has numerous benefits for physical and mental health. It reduces the risk of chronic diseases, improves cardiovascular health, and enhances cognitive function. Additionally, exercise plays a vital role in maintaining healthy body weight and promoting overall well-being.

In the podcast segment, the speaker challenges the notion that exercise is the sole contributor to good health. While acknowledging its advantages, they argue that factors such as genetics, diet, and mental well-being also play significant roles in determining overall health.

The speaker emphasizes that exercise alone cannot guarantee well-being and that a holistic approach is necessary for optimal health.

The speaker in the podcast segment supports the ideas presented in the lecture. They agree that exercise has multiple benefits and is an essential component of a healthy lifestyle. However, they challenge the notion that exercise is the sole determinant of overall well-being. By highlighting the importance of genetics, diet, and mental well-being, the speaker presents a more comprehensive view of health.

Therefore, while the lecture emphasizes exercise as a crucial aspect of promoting physical and mental health, the podcast segment adds a nuanced perspective by considering additional factors. Both sources agree on the significance of exercise but differ in their emphasis on other determinants of overall health.

Sample Integrated Writing Task - 2

Integrated Writing Task:
Read the excerpt below from a lecture on the impacts of deforestation on biodiversity, then listen to a related podcast segment. Summarize the main points made in the lecture and the podcast segment. Explain how the speaker in the podcast supports or challenges the ideas presented in the lecture.

Lecture Excerpt (reading passage):
Deforestation poses a significant threat to global biodiversity. The clearing of forests for agricultural purposes, urbanization, and logging activities has led to the loss of habitats for countless species. This loss of biodiversity not only disrupts ecosystems but also affects ecological balance and the provision of vital ecosystem services. Efforts must be made to conserve forests and promote sustainable practices to mitigate the negative impacts of deforestation.

Deforestation is an alarming issue that poses a significant threat to global biodiversity. The relentless clearing of forests, primarily driven by agricultural expansion, urbanization, and logging activities, has resulted in the loss of critical habitats for countless species worldwide. This loss of biodiversity has far-reaching consequences, deeply affecting ecosystems, ecological balance, and the provision of crucial ecosystem services.

Forests are home to an incredible variety of plant and animal species, many of which are endemic and found nowhere else on Earth. The destruction of their habitats has severe repercussions, disrupting complex ecological interactions and jeopardizing the delicate balance of ecosystems. With the loss of species, the functionality of these ecosystems is compromised, leading to reduced resilience and potential ecosystem collapses.

Furthermore, deforestation impairs the provision of vital ecosystem services on which human societies depend. Forests play a crucial role in regulating climate by absorbing carbon dioxide and releasing oxygen, mitigating the impacts of climate change. They also provide essential resources such as clean water, soil fertility, and natural medicines. The destruction of forests not only compromises these services but can also lead to increased soil erosion, water pollution, and decreased availability of resources, affecting communities that rely on forests for their livelihoods.

To mitigate the negative impacts of deforestation, urgent efforts are needed to conserve forests and promote sustainable practices. Implementing responsible land-use practices, supporting reforestation initiatives, and enforcing strict regulations against illegal logging are vital steps. Balancing economic development with conservation objectives and implementing sustainable agricultural practices, such as agroforestry and land restoration techniques, can help ensure the long-term protection of forests and their biodiversity.

In conclusion, deforestation has dire consequences for global biodiversity, affecting ecosystems, ecological balance, and the provision of critical ecosystem services. Conservation efforts and the promotion of sustainable practices are essential to mitigate the negative impacts of deforestation and preserve the invaluable benefits forests provide to both nature and human societies. Only through collective action can we secure a sustainable future, protecting both forests and the biodiversity they harbor.

Speaker transcript (podcast segment):

Host: Welcome to the podcast, where we explore various perspectives on environmental issues. Today, we have with us an expert in sustainable forestry practices to discuss the impacts of deforestation on biodiversity. Welcome, Dr. Emma Johnson.

Dr. Johnson: Thank you for having me. It's a pleasure to be here.

Host: Dr. Johnson, the lecture we just heard highlighted the detrimental effects of deforestation on biodiversity. However, could you provide us with a different perspective on this topic?

Dr. Johnson: Absolutely. While it is true that deforestation can have negative consequences for biodiversity, it's important to recognize that not all forms of deforestation are equal. Selective logging, for example, when applied with sustainable practices, can have positive outcomes. By carefully selecting specific trees for timber extraction while leaving the majority of the forest intact, we can minimize disruptions to ecosystems and maintain habitat conditions for various species.

Host: That's an interesting point. Could you elaborate on how responsible forest management practices contribute to maintaining biodiversity?

Dr. Johnson: Certainly. Responsible forest management involves restoring degraded forests and implementing techniques that promote biodiversity restoration. By ensuring the regrowth of key tree species and providing habitats for diverse flora and fauna, we can create conditions that support a thriving ecosystem. This approach not only aids biodiversity restoration but also provides economic benefits for local communities.

Host: So, it seems like responsible forest management practices can strike a balance between conserving biodiversity and supporting local livelihoods. How can we promote these practices on a larger scale?

Dr. Johnson: Education and awareness are key. By promoting the benefits of sustainable forestry practices and highlighting successful case studies, we can encourage governments, stakeholders, and communities to adopt responsible forest management techniques. It's crucial to emphasize the importance of preserving biodiversity while considering the needs of local populations. This way, we can create a sustainable future where biodiversity thrives alongside human development.

Host: Thank you, Dr. Johnson, for sharing your insights on this important topic. It's clear that responsible forest management has the potential to positively impact biodiversity and support local communities. We appreciate your expertise.

Dr. Johnson: Thank you again for having me. It was a pleasure to shed light on this perspective.

Answer:

The lecture highlights that deforestation poses a significant threat to global biodiversity. The clearing of forests for various purposes, such as agriculture and logging, leads to the loss of habitats and disrupts ecosystems. This loss of biodiversity affects ecological balance and important ecosystem services. The lecture emphasizes the need for conservation efforts and sustainable practices to mitigate the negative impacts of deforestation.

In the podcast segment, the speaker challenges the idea that all deforestation activities have detrimental effects on biodiversity. They argue that selective logging or restoring degraded forests can have positive outcomes. The speaker acknowledges the importance of conservation efforts but emphasizes that responsible and sustainable forest management practices can contribute to biodiversity restoration and provide economic benefits to local communities.

The speaker in the podcast supports the ideas presented in the lecture by endorsing the importance of conservation. However, the speaker challenges the notion that all forms of deforestation have negative consequences for biodiversity. By highlighting the potential positive outcomes of certain deforestation activities when managed sustainably, the speaker expands on the possibilities of balancing biodiversity preservation and economic development.

Therefore, while the lecture emphasizes the negative impacts of deforestation on biodiversity, the podcast segment adds a nuanced perspective by highlighting the potential positive outcomes of specific forms of deforestation with responsible management practices. Both sources agree on the significance of biodiversity conservation but differ in their stance on the potential outcomes of certain deforestation activities.

Sample Integrated Writing Task - 3

Integrated Writing Task:

Read the excerpt below from a lecture on the impacts of deforestation on biodiversity, then listen to a related podcast segment. Summarize the main points made in the lecture and the podcast segment. Explain how the speaker in the podcast supports or challenges the ideas presented in the lecture.

Lecture:

Climate change is a pressing issue that affects various aspects of our environment, and coral reefs are particularly vulnerable to its effects.

The rising global temperatures associated with climate change pose a significant threat to coral reefs. Increased ocean temperatures can trigger a phenomenon known as coral bleaching, whereby corals expel the algae living within them, causing them to lose their vibrant colors and become more susceptible to disease and death. Widespread bleaching events have been observed in recent years, leading to extensive coral mortality and subsequent decline in reef health.

But it's not just rising temperatures that are impacting coral reefs. The absorption of excess carbon dioxide by the oceans is causing them to become more acidic, a process known as ocean acidification. This acidification hampers the ability of corals and other marine organisms to build their calcium carbonate structures, making it harder for reefs to recover from disturbances and inhibiting their growth.

In addition to these climate-related impacts, rising sea levels due to global warming pose a threat to coral reefs by altering the water depths they can thrive in. Shifts in coastal ecosystems and increased sedimentation can smother corals and limit their access to sunlight, further compounding the challenges they face.

In light of these threats, urgent action is required. Mitigating climate change through the reduction of greenhouse gas emissions is key to minimizing the long-term impacts on coral reefs. However, we must also address other stressors that contribute to their decline, such as pollution runoff from land-based activities and overfishing. By taking a comprehensive approach that tackles both global and local stressors, we can enhance the resilience of coral reefs and promote their long-term survival.

In conclusion, climate change poses significant challenges to coral reefs through rising temperatures, ocean acidification, and sea-level rise. However, by addressing these impacts and taking action to mitigate climate change, alongside efforts to address local stressors, we can help protect and restore these vital ecosystems. The preservation of coral reefs is not just important for their beauty and biodiversity, but also for the critical services they provide to coastal communities and broader marine ecosystems.

Podcast Segment:

Host: Welcome to our podcast, where we explore different perspectives on environmental conservation. Today, we have with us an expert in marine ecology to discuss the impacts of climate change on coral reefs. Welcome, Dr. Sarah Thompson.

Dr. Thompson: Thank you for having me. I'm excited to be here and discuss this important topic.

Host: Dr. Thompson, the lecture we just read highlighted the significant threats that climate change poses to coral reefs. Could you provide a different perspective on this issue?

Dr. Thompson: Certainly. While climate change does play a significant role in the decline of coral reefs, it's important to recognize that there are other factors contributing to their degradation. Pollution, overfishing, and coastal development are some of the local stressors that also pose threats to coral reef ecosystems. These factors can weaken corals' resilience to climate change impacts and exacerbate their decline.

Host: That's an interesting perspective. Could you elaborate on how addressing these local stressors alongside climate change mitigation efforts can protect and restore coral reefs?

Dr. Thompson: Absolutely. It is crucial to recognize that protecting and restoring coral reefs requires a comprehensive approach. While climate change mitigation is vital, addressing local stressors is equally important. Reducing pollution and improving coastal management can help reduce coral reef degradation and support their recovery. This comprehensive approach helps create more resilient ecosystems that can better withstand the impacts of climate change.

Host: So, it seems like considering both global and local stressors is key in coral reef conservation. How can we promote such comprehensive measures on a broader scale?

Dr. Thompson: Education and awareness are essential in promoting comprehensive coral reef conservation efforts. By providing information about the interconnectedness of global and local stressors, we can empower individuals, communities, and policymakers to take action.

Collaboration between stakeholders, governments, and conservation organizations is crucial in implementing effective strategies that address both climate change and local stressors. By integrating these approaches, we can ensure the long-term protection and restoration of coral reef ecosystems.

Host: Thank you, Dr. Thompson, for sharing your insights on this important topic. It's clear that considering both global and local stressors is vital in safeguarding coral reef ecosystems. We appreciate your expertise.

Dr. Thompson: Thank you for having me. It was a pleasure to contribute to the discussion.

Answer:

Both the lecture and the podcast segment discuss the impacts of climate change on coral reefs while highlighting the importance of addressing both global and local stressors for their conservation and restoration.

In the lecture, it is emphasized that rising global temperatures associated with climate change pose a significant threat to coral reefs. This leads to coral bleaching, ocean acidification, and rising sea levels, all of which contribute to the decline of coral reef ecosystems. The urgent need to mitigate climate change through the reduction of greenhouse gas emissions is highlighted, along with the importance of addressing other stressors such as pollution runoff and overfishing to enhance reef resilience.

The podcast segment adds a different perspective by acknowledging that while climate change plays a significant role, local stressors also contribute to coral reef degradation. It highlights pollution, overfishing, and coastal development as additional threats that weaken coral resilience to climate change impacts. The speaker emphasizes the importance of addressing these local stressors in conjunction with climate change mitigation efforts to support coral reef recovery and create more resilient ecosystems.

Both the lecture and the podcast segment agree on the need for a comprehensive approach to coral reef conservation. Education, awareness, and collaboration among stakeholders, governments, and conservation organizations are critical in implementing effective strategies. By integrating efforts to mitigate climate change and address local stressors such as pollution and overfishing, we can promote the long-term protection and restoration of coral reef ecosystems.

In conclusion, the lecture and podcast segment present a holistic understanding of the threats to coral reefs posed by climate change and local stressors. They emphasize the need to address both global and local factors through collaboration and comprehensive measures, ensuring the preservation and resilience of coral reef ecosystems.

Sample Integrated Writing Task - 4

Integrated Writing Task:

Read the excerpt below from a lecture on the impacts of noise pollution on marine life, then listen to a related podcast segment. Summarize the main points made in the lecture and the podcast segment. Explain how the speaker in the podcast supports or challenges the ideas presented in the lecture.

Lecture:

Noise pollution has detrimental effects on marine life, particularly marine mammals and fish. Underwater noise, primarily caused by human activities such as shipping, military exercises, and offshore construction, disrupts the natural acoustic environment of the ocean. It can lead to changes in behavior, communication interference, hearing damage, and even physical harm to marine species. Urgent measures are needed to mitigate and regulate underwater noise pollution to protect marine ecosystems.

Noise pollution poses a significant threat to marine life, especially marine mammals and fish, with dire consequences for marine ecosystems. Human activities such as shipping, military exercises, and offshore construction generate underwater noise that disrupts the natural acoustic environment of the ocean. This disruption can have far-reaching impacts on marine species.

The effects of underwater noise pollution on marine life are detrimental. It can lead to changes in behavior, including altered feeding patterns, migration routes, and breeding habits.

Communication interference becomes prevalent, as animals rely on sound for vital activities such as finding mates and locating food sources. Continuous exposure to high-intensity noise can cause chronic stress, impairing the overall health of marine species.

Hearing damage is a severe consequence of noise pollution for many marine organisms. Prolonged exposure to loud noise levels can lead to permanent hearing loss, impacting their ability to communicate, navigate, and avoid predators. Additionally, physical harm can occur, such as injuries due to the displacement caused by high-intensity noise, or direct damage to delicate tissues in the auditory system.

To safeguard marine ecosystems, urgent measures are required to mitigate and regulate underwater noise pollution. Implementing regulations to limit noise emissions from human activities, creating marine protected areas with reduced noise impact, and developing technology that reduces underwater noise levels are crucial steps. Collaborative efforts between policymakers, industry stakeholders, and environmental organizations are necessary to raise awareness, enforce regulations, and promote sustainable practices that prioritize the protection of marine ecosystems.

In conclusion, noise pollution has profound and damaging effects on marine life. Human activities generating underwater noise disrupt the natural acoustic environment of the ocean, severely impacting marine mammals and fish. Immediate action is necessary to mitigate and regulate noise pollution through strict regulations and collaborative efforts, ensuring the long- term survival and health of marine ecosystems.

Podcast Segment:

Host: Welcome back to our podcast series on environmental issues. Today, we will be discussing the impacts of noise pollution on marine life. Joining us is Dr. Mark Wilson, an expert in marine biology. Welcome, Dr. Wilson.

Dr. Wilson: Thank you for having me. I'm delighted to be here.

Host: Dr. Wilson, the lecture we just heard emphasized the negative effects of noise pollution on marine life. Could you provide a different perspective on this issue?

Dr. Wilson: Certainly. While it is undeniable that noise pollution has adverse effects on marine life, it's important to consider the context and potential variation in its impacts. While some species are highly sensitive to noise disturbances, others have shown more resilience and adaptation. Additionally, more research is needed to fully understand the long-term consequences of noise pollution on different marine organisms and ecosystems.

Host: That's an interesting viewpoint. Could you elaborate on any specific examples or studies that support this alternative perspective?

Dr. Wilson: Absolutely. For instance, certain marine mammal species have been observed adapting their behavior patterns to avoid noise sources, such as shifting their vocalizations or altering their migration routes. Additionally, studies have shown differences in the sensitivity and reaction of various fish species to underwater noise. Some exhibit stronger responses, while others seem to be less affected.

Host: So, it seems like there may be variability in the impacts of noise pollution on marine life. How does this perspective influence conservation efforts?

Dr. Wilson: Recognizing the variability in species' responses to noise pollution is crucial for effective conservation strategies. It highlights the need for tailored approaches and further research to better understand the specific impacts on different species and ecosystems. By considering this variation, we can develop targeted mitigation measures, such as implementing quiet zones or adjusting human activities to minimize disturbance in sensitive areas.

Host: Thank you, Dr. Wilson, for sharing this alternative perspective on noise pollution and its effects on marine life. It's clear that understanding species-specific responses and investing in further research is essential for conservation efforts.

Dr. Wilson: Thank you for having me. It was a pleasure to contribute to the discussion.

Answer:

In the lecture, the detrimental effects of noise pollution on marine life, particularly marine mammals and fish, due to human activities such as shipping and offshore construction, were emphasized. The lecture highlighted how underwater noise disrupts the natural acoustic environment of the ocean, leading to behavioral changes, communication interference, hearing damage, and physical harm to marine species. It stressed the urgency for mitigating noise pollution to protect marine ecosystems.

The podcast segment provided an alternative perspective on noise pollution and its impacts on marine life. Dr. Wilson acknowledged the negative effects but emphasized the potential variation in species' responses and adaptation to noise disturbances. The podcast speaker pointed out that certain marine mammals and fish have shown resilience and the ability to adapt their behavior patterns to avoid noise sources. They highlighted that more research is needed to fully understand the long-term consequences of noise pollution on different marine organisms and ecosystems.

Therefore, the podcast speaker supports the ideas presented in the lecture by indicating that some species have exhibited adaptive responses to noise pollution. Their perspective complements the lecture by emphasizing the need to consider variation in species' reactions and conduct further research to develop targeted conservation strategies. This integrated approach can help mitigate the impacts of noise pollution on marine life and preserve marine ecosystems more effectively.

Sample Integrated Writing Task - 5

Integrated Writing Task:

Read the excerpt below from a lecture on the benefits of green spaces in urban areas, then listen to a related podcast segment. Summarize the main points made in the lecture and the podcast segment. Explain how the speaker in the podcast supports or challenges the ideas presented in the lecture.

Lecture:

Green spaces in urban areas provide numerous benefits to both people and the environment. They contribute to improved air quality by acting as natural filters, absorbing pollutants and releasing oxygen. Green spaces also help mitigate the urban heat island effect, reducing temperatures and providing cool areas for relaxation and recreation. Additionally, these spaces offer opportunities for physical activity, stress reduction, and social interactions, enhancing the overall well-being and quality of life for urban residents. The preservation and creation of green spaces are vital for sustainable urban development.

Green spaces play a vital role in improving the well-being of both people and the environment. Let's delve into the importance of these urban oases and how they contribute to sustainable urban development. Firstly, green spaces have a significant impact on air quality. They act as natural filters, absorbing pollutants and releasing oxygen, thereby improving the overall air quality in urban areas. This reduction in air pollution has direct health benefits for residents, resulting in improved respiratory health and a lower risk of respiratory diseases.

Secondly, green spaces help mitigate the urban heat island effect. In highly built-up areas, concrete and asphalt absorb and radiate heat, causing higher temperatures. However, the presence of green spaces helps to cool the surroundings. Trees and vegetation provide shade and evaporative cooling, reducing ambient temperatures and providing relief during hot summer months. This helps create more comfortable outdoor spaces for people to relax and engage in various activities.

Furthermore, green spaces offer opportunities for physical activity, stress reduction, and social interaction. Accessible parks, gardens, and recreational spaces within urban environments encourage people to engage in outdoor activities, promoting physical fitness and overall well-being. These green spaces also serve as tranquil settings, providing a respite from the hustle and bustle of city life and contributing to stress reduction. In addition, they create opportunities for social interactions, fostering a sense of community and connection among urban dwellers.

Preservation and creation of green spaces are of utmost importance for sustainable urban development. Cities must allocate land and resources for the establishment and maintenance of green spaces. Initiatives such as urban forestry programs, rooftop gardens, and community gardens can help integrate greenery into urban landscapes. Additionally, urban planning should consider equitable distribution of green spaces, ensuring that all neighborhoods have access to these essential resources.

In conclusion, green spaces in urban areas offer a range of benefits to residents and the environment alike. They contribute to improved air quality, mitigate the urban heat island effect, promote physical well-being, and facilitate social interactions. The preservation and creation of green spaces should be a priority in urban planning efforts, ensuring that cities remain sustainable and livable for present and future generations.

Podcast Segment:

Host: Welcome to our podcast, where we explore the importance of green spaces in urban areas. Joining us today is Dr. Lisa Anderson, an expert in urban planning.

Welcome, Dr. Anderson.

Dr. Anderson: Thank you for having me. I'm excited to be here.

Host: Dr. Anderson, the lecture we just heard emphasized the benefits of green spaces in urban areas. Can you provide a different perspective on this topic?

Dr. Anderson: Absolutely. While the lecture highlighted important aspects, it's essential to recognize that the benefits of green spaces can vary depending on the specific context and design. Not all green spaces provide the same levels of ecosystem services or social benefits. Factors such as size, location, and maintenance can significantly influence their effectiveness.

Host: That's an interesting viewpoint. Can you provide an example or expand further on these variations?

Dr. Anderson: Certainly. For instance, larger green spaces such as parks or urban forests tend to offer greater air purification and temperature regulation compared to small pocket parks. The accessibility and distribution of green spaces play a critical role in social benefits, as residents in closer proximity can enjoy a wider range of amenities and engage in regular physical activity.

Additionally, the design and management of green spaces should consider factors like cultural appropriateness and community engagement to ensure they cater to the diverse needs of urban populations.

Host: So, it seems that the effectiveness of green spaces depends on various factors. How does this perspective influence urban planning efforts?

Dr. Anderson: Recognizing the variations in the benefits of green spaces is essential in urban planning. It emphasizes the need for careful consideration of factors such as size, location, connectivity, and community engagement. Urban planners should aim for a mix of green spaces that address specific needs and support multiple ecosystem services. This approach ensures that green spaces contribute effectively to air quality improvement, urban heat reduction, physical well-being, and social cohesion.

Host: Thank you, Dr. Anderson, for sharing this alternative perspective on the benefits of green spaces in urban areas. It's clear that considering variations and tailoring green space design to meet specific local contexts and community needs are crucial for successful urban planning efforts.

Dr. Anderson: Thank you for having me. I hope this discussion encourages urban planners to maximize the potential benefits of green spaces while creating more sustainable and livable urban environments.

Answer:

In the lecture, the benefits of green spaces in urban areas were emphasized, highlighting their contributions to improved air quality, urban heat reduction, physical well-being, and social interactions. The lecture stressed the need for the preservation and creation of green spaces for sustainable urban development.

The podcast segment provided an alternative perspective, acknowledging the benefits of green spaces but emphasizing the importance of considering variations. Dr. Anderson pointed out that not all green spaces offer the same levels of ecosystem services or social benefits. Factors such as size, location, and maintenance significantly influence the effectiveness of green spaces. They highlighted that larger green spaces tend to provide greater air purification and temperature regulation, while design and community engagement play a role in social benefits.

Therefore, the podcast speaker supports the ideas presented in the lecture by recognizing the variations in the benefits of green spaces and emphasizing the need for tailored urban planning efforts. Their perspective complements the lecture by emphasizing the importance of considering factors such as size, location, connectivity, and community engagement in green space design.

This integrated approach can lead to more effective urban planning efforts, ensuring that green spaces meet the specific needs of diverse urban populations and contribute to sustainable and livable environments.

Grammar for the TOEFL

To excel in the TOEFL test, high-performing students must have a solid understanding of essential English grammar concepts and rules. Below is a concise summary of key grammatical points critical for success in the TOEFL exam.

1. **Verb Tenses:** Mastering the various verb tenses is fundamental. Understand the distinctions between present simple, present continuous, present perfect, past simple, past continuous, past perfect, future simple, and future perfect to accurately convey different time frames in speaking and writing.

2. **Subject-Verb Agreement:** Ensure that verbs agree with their subjects in number (singular or plural). Watch for exceptions with collective nouns, indefinite pronouns, and tricky subjects connected by conjunctions.

3. **Sentence Structure:** Develop competence in sentence structure by understanding the components of a sentence (subject, verb, and object). Practice crafting simple, compound, and complex sentences accurately and coherently.

4. **Modifiers:** Recognize and correctly use modifiers, including adjectives and adverbs, to provide precise descriptions and add details to sentences. Maintain parallelism when using multiple modifiers to ensure clarity and coherence.

5. **Articles:** Understand the distinctions between definite (the) and indefinite (a/an) articles. Learn when and how to use articles with countable and uncountable nouns, as well as in specific and general contexts.

6. **Pronouns:** Familiarize yourself with personal pronouns (I, you, he/she/it, we, they), possessive pronouns (mine, yours, his/hers/its, ours, theirs), and reflexive/intensive pronouns (myself, yourself, himself/herself/itself, ourselves, themselves).

7. **Prepositions:** Master the proper use of prepositions in different contexts (time, place, manner, and purpose) to accurately convey relationships between words and phrases. Practice common prepositions such as in, on, at, by, and with.

8. **Comparative and Superlative Forms:** Understand the proper structure and usage of comparative (-er) and superlative (-est) forms, as well as irregular forms, to describe and compare things, people, or qualities.

9. **Conditionals:** Comprehend conditional sentence structures (zero, first, second, third, and mixed conditionals) to express hypothetical situations and their possible outcomes accurately.

10. **Word Order:** Master word order rules, such as subject-verb-object (SVO) pattern, to form grammatically correct sentences. Pay attention to inversion in interrogative forms and the placement of adjectives, adverbs, and indirect/direct objects.

11. **Gerunds and Infinitives:** Understand how to use gerunds (verb + -ing) and infinitives (to + verb) as nouns, objects, or complements in a sentence. Learn patterns and verbs that require specific forms.

12. **Relative Clauses:** Comprehend relative pronouns (who, whom, whose, which, that) and relative adverbs (where, when, why) to create meaningful and grammatically correct relative clauses that provide additional information about a noun.

English grammar encompasses various components that contribute to effective communication. By understanding key aspects such as nouns, verbs, adjectives, tenses, and sentence structure, learners can attain proficiency in using these grammatical elements correctly and coherently. The following concise overview aims to provide a comprehensive explanation, supported by examples.

1. **Nouns:** Nouns are words that represent people, places, things, or ideas. They can be classified as common (e.g., book, city) or proper (e.g., Mary, London). Nouns can also be categorized as countable (e.g., two books) or uncountable (e.g., water). In sentences, nouns can function as subjects (e.g., Mary reads a book), objects (e.g., John saw Mary), or possessives (e.g., the dog's tail).

2. **Verbs:** Verbs are action or state-of-being words that express actions, events, or conditions. They can be divided into main verbs and auxiliary (helping) verbs. Main verbs indicate the central action (e.g., run, think), while auxiliary verbs support the main verb to express tense, mood, or voice (e.g., do, have). Verbs change form based on tense (e.g., present, past), such as "He plays soccer" (present) or "She played piano" (past).

3. **Adjectives:** Adjectives modify nouns or pronouns by describing or quantifying them. They provide additional information about qualities, characteristics, or quantities. For example, in the sentence "The blue sky is clear," "blue" describes the color of the sky, while "clear" describes its condition.

4. **Tenses:** Tenses indicate the time of an action or state. English has various tenses, including past, present, and future, which can be further divided into simple, continuous, perfect, or perfect continuous forms. For instance, in the sentence "She will be singing tomorrow," "will be singing" represents the future continuous tense.

5. **Sentence Structure:** Sentence structure involves the arrangement of words within a sentence to convey meaning. Basic sentence structure follows a subject-verb-object (SVO) pattern, such as "She (subject) plays (verb) the piano (object)." However, sentence structure can be more complex, incorporating additional elements such as adverbs (e.g., "She plays the piano beautifully") or dependent clauses (e.g., "After she finished her homework, she played the piano").

These examples highlight key grammar components in English. However, mastering grammar extends beyond the understanding of isolated concepts. It involves recognizing and applying grammar rules in various contexts, which necessitates extensive practice and exposure to authentic English materials.

Vocabulary for the TOEFL

1. Abundant (adj.) - existing in large quantities; plentiful. Example: The rainforest is abundant with diverse plant and animal species.

2. Acquire (v.) - to obtain or gain possession of something. Example: She hopes to acquire valuable skills through her internship.

3. Adapt (v.) - to adjust or modify in order to fit new circumstances or conditions. Example: The business had to adapt its strategies to meet changing market demands.

4. Adequate (adj.) - satisfactory or sufficient in quality or quantity. Example: The student's answer was adequate, addressing all the required points.

5. Ambiguous (adj.) - having more than one possible interpretation or meaning. Example: The politician made an ambiguous statement, leaving the audience confused.

6. Analyze (v.) - to examine or evaluate in detail, typically to understand its structure or nature. Example: The researcher analyzed the data to identify patterns and trends.

7. Appropriate (adj.) - suitable or proper in the circumstances. Example: He found it inappropriate to wear casual attire to a formal event.

8. Assert (v.) - to state or declare confidently or forcefully. Example: The author asserts that education is the key to societal progress.

9. Authentic (adj.) - genuine; real; not counterfeit or copied. Example: The museum displayed authentic artifacts from ancient civilizations.

10. Benefit (n.) - an advantage or positive outcome gained from something. Example: Exercise has numerous health benefits, including increased stamina and improved mood.

11. Cite (v.) - to quote as evidence or support for a statement or argument. Example: The student cited several scholarly articles to back up their research findings.

12. Clarify (v.) - to make clear or understandable by explaining or providing additional information. Example: The teacher clarified the concept by giving real-life examples.

13. Coherent (adj.) - logical and consistent; making sense as a whole. Example: The speaker presented a coherent argument that supported their thesis.

14. Compelling (adj.) - evoking interest, attention, or admiration in a captivating or persuasive manner. Example: The novel had a compelling storyline that kept readers engaged till the end.

15. Contribute (v.) - to offer or provide one's share or resources to a common purpose or cause. Example: The volunteer's efforts greatly contributed to the success of the charity event.

16. Core (adj.) - fundamental or essential; forming the central part of something. Example: Math and language skills are core components of early childhood education.

17. Counter (v.) - to respond to an action with an opposing or contrary one. Example: The company introduced price cuts to counter its competitors' discounts.

18. Credible (adj.) - believable and reliable; worthy of trust and confidence. Example: The witness provided a credible account of the events that occurred.

19. Critique (n.) - a detailed analysis, evaluation, or review of something, often expressing both positive and negative aspects. Example: The film received mixed critique from critics, with some praising the acting and others criticizing the plot.

20. Deduce (v.) - to infer or conclude something through logical reasoning or evidence. Example: From the footprints, the detective deduced that someone had recently entered the room.

21. Demonstrate (v.) - to show or make evident by providing proof or evidence. Example: The experiment demonstrated the relationship between temperature and pressure.

22. Depict (v.) - to represent or portray something or someone in a particular manner or through description. Example: The painting vividly depicted the beauty of the countryside.

23. Derive (v.) - to obtain or receive (something) from a specified source. Example: She derived inspiration from her favorite authors when writing her own book.

24. Distinguish (v.) - to recognize or perceive as different or distinct. Example: His unique painting style helps him distinguish himself from other artists.

25. Elaborate (adj.) - detailed, intricate, or developed with many parts or aspects. Example: The architect presented an elaborate plan for the new building design.

26. Emerge (v.) - to become apparent, evident, or visible; to come into existence. Example: The sun emerged from behind the clouds, casting a warm light over the landscape.

27. Emphasize (v.) - to give special importance or significance to something. Example: The teacher emphasized the importance of studying for the upcoming exam.

28. Enable (v.) - to give someone the means, authority, or capability to do or achieve something. Example: The new software program enables users to perform complex calculations with ease.

29. Enhance (v.) - to improve or increase the quality, value, or attractiveness of something. Example: Adding fresh herbs can enhance the flavor of a dish.

30. Evolve (v.) - to develop or change gradually over time. Example: The technology industry constantly evolves as new innovations emerge.

31. Excerpt (n.) - a short extract or passage taken from a longer piece of writing, music, or film. Example: The historian discussed an interesting excerpt from a letter written by a famous author.

32. Exploit (v.) - to make full use of or take advantage of something for personal gain or benefit. Example: Some companies exploit cheap labor to maximize their profits.

33. Expose (v.) - to make visible, reveal, or bring to light something that was hidden or secret. Example: The journalist exposed a corruption scandal within the government.

34. Facilitate (v.) - to make a process or task easier or smoother; to assist or enable. Example: The new software will facilitate communication among team members.

35. Fluctuate (v.) - to change or vary irregularly or unpredictably. Example: The stock market can fluctuate based on various economic factors.

36. Foster (v.) - to encourage or promote the development or growth of something. Example: The organization works to foster a sense of community among its members.

37. Generate (v.) - to produce, create, or bring into existence. Example: Wind turbines generate electricity from the power of the wind.

38. Grasp (v.) - to understand, perceive, or comprehend something fully or firmly. Example: It took her a while to grasp the concept, but she finally understood it.

39. Highlight (v.) - to emphasize or draw attention to something important or a significant detail. Example: The presenter used visual aids to highlight the key points of the presentation.

40. Hypothesize (v.) - to suggest or speculate a possible explanation or solution based on limited evidence. Example: The scientist hypothesized that the experiment's results were influenced by temperature.

41. Illuminate (v.) - to provide light or brightness; to clarify or explain a complex concept or idea. Example: The professor used examples to illuminate the challenging topic.

42. Imply (v.) - to suggest or indicate something without explicitly stating it. Example: His silence implied that he did not agree with the proposal.

43. Incline (v.) - to have a tendency or preference to act or think in a particular way. Example: She has always had an incline to pursue a career in medicine.

44. Infer (v.) - to deduce or conclude from evidence or reasoning rather than from explicit statements. Example: Based on the evidence presented, we can infer that the suspect was at the crime scene.

45. Isolate (v.) - to separate or set apart from others; to be alone or detached.

46. Example: The researchers successfully isolated the specific gene responsible for the trait.

47. Justify (v.) - to provide reasons, explanations, or evidence to support a statement or action. Example: The lawyer presented evidence to justify her client's innocence.

48. Maintain (v.) - to keep in the same condition, state, or position over a period of time. Example: Regular exercise and a balanced diet can help maintain good health.

49. Manipulate (v.) - to handle, control, or influence skillfully in a cunning or unscrupulous manner. Example: The politician was accused of manipulating public opinion for personal gain.

50. Negate (v.) - to nullify, deny, or make ineffective; to contradict or prove false. Example: The evidence presented negates the initial claims made by the defendant.

51. Observe (v.) - to notice, watch, or perceive carefully; to follow established rules or customs. Example: It is important to observe proper etiquette when attending a formal event.

52. Overlook (v.) - to fail to notice or consider something; to disregard or ignore. Example: The supervisor overlooked several mistakes in the report.

53. Perceive (v.) - to become aware of or understand through the senses or intuition. Example: She perceived a change in his attitude, indicating something was wrong.

54. Persuade (v.) - to convince or influence someone to do or believe something through reasoning or argument. Example: The speaker used compelling evidence to persuade the audience to support the cause.

55. Portray (v.) - to depict or represent someone or something in a particular way. Example: The artist portrayed the tranquility of the landscape in her painting.

56. Predict (v.) - to foretell or forecast future events or outcomes based on information or evidence. Example: The scientist used data and mathematical models to predict climate patterns.

57. Presume (v.) - to assume or suppose something is true without conclusive evidence. Example: We presumed he was guilty, but it turned out to be a misunderstanding.

58. Probe (v.) - to investigate or explore carefully or thoroughly. Example: The detective carefully probed the crime scene for any clues.

59. Recall (v.) - to remember or bring back to mind something from the past. Example: She couldn't recall where she had left her keys.

60. Recount (v.) - to tell someone in detail an event or experience previously witnessed or undergone. Example: The survivor recounted the terrifying ordeal of being lost at sea.

61. Reflect (v.) - to think about or consider something deeply; to mirror or show an image. Example: The students were asked to reflect on their learning experiences.

62. Reinforce (v.) - to strengthen or support with additional evidence, statements, or actions. Example: The trainer used positive feedback to reinforce good behavior.

63. Relate (v.) - to establish a connection or link between two or more things; to tell a story or give an account. Example: She related her personal experiences to illustrate the importance of perseverance.

64. Replicate (v.) - to copy, reproduce, or duplicate something exactly. Example: The scientist replicated the experiment to confirm the initial findings.

65. Retain (v.) - to keep or hold in possession, use, or memory. Example: It is important to retain the knowledge learned throughout the course.

66. Reveal (v.) - to disclose or make known something that was previously hidden or secret. Example: The investigation revealed the identity of the culprit.

67. Specify (v.) - to state, describe, or identify precisely or in detail. Example: Please specify the exact time and location of the meeting.

68. Sustain (v.) - to maintain or prolong; to bear the weight or pressure of something. Example: Renewable energy sources help sustain a cleaner and greener environment.

69. Synthesize (v.) - to combine diverse elements or ideas into a coherent whole or understanding. Example: The researcher synthesized the various theories to propose a new hypothesis.

70. Transform (v.) - to make a significant change in form, appearance, or nature. Example: The invention of smartphones has transformed the way we communicate.

71. Undermine (v.) - to weaken or compromise the effectiveness, power, or stability of something. Example: His actions undermined the trust that had been built within the team.

72. Validate (v.) - to prove or demonstrate something as true, valid, or acceptable. Example: The experiment's results validated the hypothesis proposed by the scientist.

73. Verify (v.) - to confirm or establish the truth, accuracy, or validity of something. Example: The technician verified the integrity of the data by conducting multiple tests.

74. Yield (v.) - to produce or provide a result, outcome, or supply. Example: The project yielded positive results, exceeding our expectations.

75. Apprehensive (adj.) - anxious or fearful about the future or a particular event. Example: She was apprehensive about speaking in public but gained confidence over time.

76. Capable (adj.) - having the ability, skill, or capacity to do something. Example: With proper training, he is capable of solving complex mathematical problems.

77. Comprehensive (adj.) - complete, thorough, and including everything that is necessary. Example: The textbook provides a comprehensive overview of the subject matter.

78. Conscientious (adj.) - diligent, careful, and thorough in one's work or duties. Example: The employee is known for being conscientious and always meeting deadlines.

79. Correlate (v.) - to have a mutual relationship or connection; to show a strong association between two or more things. Example: The study found a strong correlation between sleep deprivation and poor academic performance.

80. Crucial (adj.) - of great importance; absolutely necessary. Example: Attention to detail is crucial in the field of medicine.

81. Cumulative (adj.) - gradually increasing or growing through successive additions. Example: The cumulative effect of regular exercise is improved cardiovascular health.

82. Evident (adj.) - clearly seen, understood, or perceived; obvious. Example: The success of the project was evident from the positive feedback received.

83. Explicit (adj.) - stated clearly and in detail, leaving no room for confusion or doubt. Example: The instructions were explicit, ensuring everyone understood the task.

84. Inherent (adj.) - existing as a natural or essential part of something; intrinsic. Example: The artist has an inherent talent for capturing emotions in her paintings.

85. Integral (adj.) - necessary or essential to make something whole or complete. Example: Communication is integral to building strong relationships.

86. Intrinsic (adj.) - belonging naturally; inherent and essential. Example: Curiosity is an intrinsic quality that drives scientific discovery.

87. Justifiable (adj.) - able to be defended or shown to be reasonable or right. Example: His decision to drop out of college was justifiable given the circumstances.

88. Lucid (adj.) - clear and easily understandable; expressed in a straightforward manner. Example: The professor's lecture was lucid, making complex concepts easy to grasp.

89. Paradoxical (adj.) - seemingly contradictory or absurd, but in fact, may be true or have a rational explanation. Example: The concept of time travel is often considered paradoxical.

90. Profound (adj.) - having deep meaning or significance; profound thoughts or ideas evoke strong emotions or intellectual stimulation. Example: The speaker's profound words moved the audience to tears.

91. Robust (adj.) - strong, healthy, and vigorous; characterized by strength and resilience. Example: The research study included a robust sample size to ensure accurate results.

92. Substantial (adj.) - of considerable importance, size, or worth; significant in amount or degree. Example: She received a substantial scholarship to attend the university.

93. **Ubiquitous (adj.)** - present, appearing, or found everywhere. Example: Smartphones have become ubiquitous in today's society.

94. **Unambiguous (adj.)** - clear and easy to understand; not open to interpretation or doubt. Example: The instructions were unambiguous, leaving no room for confusion.

95. **Unprecedented (adj.)** - never before known or experienced; exceptional or unparalleled. Example: The pandemic has caused unprecedented disruptions to the global economy.

96. **Vibrant (adj.)** - full of energy, enthusiasm, and life; characterized by brightness and vivid colors. Example: The vibrant atmosphere of the carnival was infectious, spreading joy to everyone.

97. **Widespread (adj.)** - existing or happening over a large area or among many people. Example: The flu outbreak was widespread, affecting communities across the region.

98. **Accessible (adj.)** - easily approached, reached, or obtained; available for use or entry. Example: The new building has accessible entrances for people with disabilities.

99. **Comprehensive (adj.)** - including or dealing with all or nearly all elements or aspects of something. Example: The comprehensive report provided a detailed analysis of the company's financial performance.

100. **Enduring (adj.)** - continuing or persisting over a long period; not easily eradicated or destroyed. Example: The enduring love between the couple lasted for decades.

101. **Proficiency (n.)** - a high degree of competence, skill, or expertise in a particular area. Example: She achieved a high level of proficiency in speaking multiple languages.

This analytical list provides 101 vital TOEFL vocabulary words. It covers a wide range of essential terms that are frequently encountered in the TOEFL test. Mastering these words will greatly contribute to success in various language skills tested on the exam. To further enhance vocabulary skills, students are encouraged to practice using these words in both written and spoken English contexts.

www.ingramcontent.com/pod-product-compliance
Lightning Source LLC
LaVergne TN
LVHW070530070526
838199LV00075B/6750